6

Status of Social Sciences in the Vernacular Languages in North East India

Editors

J.P. Singh
D.R. Syiemlieh
C.J. Thomas

Regency Publications
New Delhi

Division of
DAYA PUBLISHING HOUSE
4760-61/23, Ansari Road,
Darya Ganj, New Delhi - 110 002
Phone: 23245578, 23244987; Fax: (011) 23260116
E-mail: info@regency-books.com
Website: www.regencybooks.com

ISBN 81-87498-15-3

Published by Regency Publications, 20/36-G, Old Market, West Patel Nagar, New Delhi 110 008 for Indian Council of Social Science Research — North-Eastern Regional Centre, Shillong, and Printed at Radiant Printers, New Delhi 110 008, Phones: 571 2539, 574 0038; Telefax: 578 3571.

Website: www.regencypublications.com
Email: regencypublications@satyam.net.in and info@regencypublicatins.com

To the
Sacred Memory
of
Late Prof. B. Pakem

FOREWORD

North Eastern Regional Centre of the Indian Council of Social Science Research decided to celebrate the 50th year of the country's independence in 1998 by organising a one day Seminar on Trends in Social Sciences and Humanities in North East India (1947-97), (Delhi, 1998). The Seminar was held on 30th March 1998. After the seminar was over we thought of holding another one day Seminar, later the same year, on the Status of Social Sciences in the Vernacular Languages of North East India.

North East India covering the States of Arunachal Pradesh, Assam, Manipur, Meghalaya, Mizoram, Nagaland and Tripura is inhabited by people who speak a number of languages. Leaving aside the large number of languages spoken by the tribes and sub-tribes in different States, there are several major languages also spoken in the region. These include Asamiya, Bengali, Hindi, Nepali, Manipuri, Khasi-Jaintia, Garo, Mizo and Tenyidie. All these languages are in different stages of development. It was, therefore, decided to take stock of all these languages to see and assess the progress that they have made during the period after independence.

A number of scholars spread over the Seven States of the region were identified and requested to contribute papers for the Seminar to be held later in 1998. Many of these scholars were initially very enthusiastic but as the time passed the enthusiasm slowed down. Some of the invitees did not even respond. Ultimately, we decided to go ahead and the Seminar was held on November 30, 1998. It was inaugurated by late Prof. B. Pakem, then Vice-Chancellor, NEHU, and Chairman ICSSR-NERC, Shillong.

The Status of Social Sciences in the languages of North East India as being published here has many gaps. Scholars invited to contribute papers on different subjects in different languages kept quiet to our repeated requests. We are sorry, therefore, for not being able to fill up these gaps. It is also possible that many of these languages do not have sufficient literature on Social Sciences. It is difficult, however, to be certain about it at the moment.

I take this opportunity to thank all my colleagues in the NERC and all those scholars who contributed papers and participated in the Seminar.

The papers presented at the Seminar are being published here in the hope that the remaining languages and subjects will be taken up sometime later. It will also perhaps encourage Governments concerned and scholars to join hands to remove the deficient areas in Social Sciences in the languages of their people.

Shillong
25th March 2000

Jai Prakash Singh
Hon. Director
ICSSR-NERC

PREFACE

The Seminar on the Status of Social Sciences in the Vernacular Languages of North East India was inspired by the earlier Seminar on Trends in Social Sciences and Humanities in North East India (Delhi, 1998). Like the former Seminar, it was also in celebration of the 50th year of the independence of the Country. A number of scholars were invited to contribute papers in their disciplines but most of them did not respond. It is possible that the scholars invited for the purpose may not be familiar with the academic goings on in their languages in the concerned disciplines or else they may not be satisfied with whatever little work is being done. Whatever be the reason, the fact is, that we could gather only a few scholars for this Seminar.

Altogether eight papers were received and presented at the Seminar. The paper on Tenyidie was received later. Some other scholars who had promised to submit their papers after the seminar also ultimately failed and hence this delay in the publication of these papers.

The Seminar was inaugurated by late Prof. B. Pakem, then Vice-Chancellor, NEHU, and Chairman, NERC-ICSSR, and was presided over by the Honorary Director Prof. J.P. Singh, at 10.30 AM on November 30, 1998. Ms. Cerilla Khonglah welcomed the participants and thereafter Prof. B. Pakem delivered his inaugural speech highlighting the need to take stock of the development of the vernacular languages and to take steps for their further development. Prof. J.P. Singh gave his Presidential remarks and Dr. C.J. Thomas proposed a vote of thanks.

Inaugural Session was followed by the First Academic Session at 11.30 AM and was Presided over by Prof. M. Taher. The following scholars presented their papers at this session:

Prof. D. Nath, Shri S.K. Bose, Prof. M. Taher and Dr. Amalendu Bhattacharjee. Prof. Taher gave his Presidential remarks and concluded the session at 1.45 PM.

The Second Academic Session started at 2.30 PM and was presided over by Prof. J.P. Singh. The following scholars presented their papers: Dr. D.R. Syiemlieh, Dr. L.S. Gassah, and Dr. Lianzela. Others not being present their papers were taken as read. The Presidential remarks concluded this session and Prof. J.P. Singh asked Dr. C.J. Thomas to propose a vote of thanks. Thus, the second session came to a close at 4 PM.

II

The papers presented at the seminar are being printed here in a different order. They are arranged alphabetically into Four Sections, and thereafter thematically but here also the former order is maintained. These are as follows:

I:1 Prof. M. Taher surveys 'Geographic Literature in Assamese' roughly from 1846, the year of publication of the monthly Orunodoi (Arunodaya) in Assamese. Assam scholars have published a large number of articles on different branches of geography but only a few books. The articles published also are of a general nature, therefore, the author concludes that writing on geography in Assamese is still in a stage of infancy. With the exception of climatology, agricultural geography, settlement geography, biogeography and regional planning and development, and medical geography which are not covered in newspaper and megazines most other topics are covered substantially including technical terms. It appears, therefore, that a strong background has already been prepared for the writing of standard works on different aspects of geography in Assamese.

I:2 Professor D. Nath has discussed 'Assamese Historical Writing in the Post-Independence Period: Their Extent and Scope'. Prof. Nath has not taken into account articles published in Journals and Magazines. He has also not taken into account textbooks. Nath initiates his study with the writings of S.K. Bhuyan and Benudhar Sharma. Both are regional historians and nationalists of sorts in spite of their inadequacies. Thereafter he goes on to refer to all-important works on different aspects of the history of Assam. Most eminent historians of Assam from S.K. Bhuyan to H.K. Barpujari wrote also in Assamese. Ahoms brought with them the tradition of writing history or Buranjis. In course of centuries this led to a general interest in history and encouraged many non-historians also to try their hand. Many of such historians are found wanting in objectivity and historical methodology but even then some of their works are of a high standard and together they cover a considerable volume of historical literature.

I:3 Numismatics is a source of history. Shri S.K. Bose has looked into the Assamese writing on the subject. In this case also the credit goes to Orunodoi to publish the first few articles on numismatics in Assamese. After which not many articles appeared on the subject. There are a few books in English on numismatic studies on North East India but none in Assamese.

I:4 Dr. Amalendu Bhattacharjee looks into the Folklore studies on North East India in Bengali language (1947-97). He has referred to all important books and articles. Starting with the books on the subject he goes on to list a number of important articles published in magazines and newspapers. Needless to say that he provides a good idea of the literature available in Bengali on the folklore of North East India.

II:5 Prof. M.S. Sangma discusses the Status of Garo language and surveys its development during the last two hundred years. He admits that Garo language has made but little progress in different branches of Social Sciences and humanities. He, however, provides a good account of the beginning of the written literature and its development in Garo.

II:6 Dr. D.R. Syiemlieh writes on the 'Status of Historical Writing in Khasi'. The first history work in Khasi was written and published by B.K. Sarma Roy in 1914.

after, Khasi writers have continued writing on different aspects of their history with some regularity.

II:7 Prof. L.S. Gassah concerns himself with 'Writings in Khasi Vernacular Pertaining to Socio-Political Issues: A Review'. In particular, he discusses the writings on Khasi Syiemship (Kingship?), Khasi religion, society, economy and administration.

There is very little duplication between two articles. Together they indicate that there is a vast literature on history in Khasi language. They have developed their language and literature to an extent that many other tribes of North East India have not been able to do so.

III:8 Dr. Lianzela discusses the 'Social Sciences in Mizo'. He gives an yearwise breakup of the publications in Mizo language and thereafter goes on to classify them subjectwise. He has discussed these publications, under economics, history, and political science. This write up shows that the Mizo scholarship is aware of the problem of the development of literature in social sciences and humanities and is taking up steps to remove this deficiency.

IV:9 Dr. D. Kuolie discusses the 'Development of Tenyidie: A Focus on Social Sciences'. There are but fewer books on Social Sciences in Tenyidie. It seems that the Nagas will have to take adequate steps to enrich their language and literature in the near future.

III

It is hoped that the Status of Social Sciences in the Vernacular Languages of North East India, a companion volume of the *Trends in Social Sciences and Humanities in North East India* (Delhi, 1998) will be received well by the scholarly world. Both these volumes will go a long way and will complement and supplement each other. We hope that social scientists and researchers from the North East will take note and attempt to remove the deficiencies in the languages concerned.

This book is being dedicated to late Prof. B. Pakem who served the NERC as Honorary Director (1985–90) and then its Chairman (1991–1999).

Editors

CONTENTS

LIST OF CONTRIBUTORS

1. Prof. Mohammed Taher
   Formerly Professor of Geography
   Gauhati University
   Guwahati
   Assam
2. Prof. D. Nath
   Head, Department of History
   Dibrugarh University
   Dibrugarh
   Assam
3. Shri S.K. Bose
   Author and Numismatist
   Guwahati
   Assam
4. Dr. Amalendu Bhattacharjee
   Department of Bengali
   G.C. College
   Silchar
   Assam
5. Prof. M.S. Sangma
   Pro-Vice-Chancellor
   Tura Campus, NEHU
   Tura, Garo Hills District
   Meghalaya
6. Dr. D.R. Syiemlieh
   Department of History
   NEHU
   Shillong

7. Prof. L.S. Gassah
Head, Department of Political Science
NEHU
Shillong
8. Dr. Lianzela
Department of Economics
Aizawl Campus, NEHU
Aizawl
Mizoram
9. Dr. D. Kuolie
Head, Department of Tenyidie
Nagaland University
Kohima
Nagaland

Chapter I

GEOGRAPHIC LITERATURE IN ASSAMESE

Mohammed Taher

Introduction

With the introduction of formal modern education in India in 1835 as per recommendation of Macaulay's Minutes, there occurred a sea-change in the approach to education in the country. It became necessary to publish textbooks in printed form conforming to modern secular and scientific education in the Indian vernacular languages, which had been nurtured mainly by the Christian missionaries of Europe and America since the later part of the 18th century. In the case of Assam, which was from 1826 (the year of annexation of the Brahmaputra Valley) to 1874 (the year of constitution of a separate province) a part of Bengal Presidency of British India, Bengali was introduced as the medium of instruction in the Brahmaputra Valley, where Assamese was the mother tongue of a vast majority of the indigenous population. This step was consistently opposed by the Christian missionaries, who started their evangelical work among the Assamese mass through Assamese language since about 1838. The persistent efforts of the missionaries like Miles Bronson, coupled with the representations submitted by local people like Anandaram Dhekial Phukan, could ultimately convince the British rulers and Assamese was restored as medium of instruction in the

Brahmaputra Valley as per resolution of the General Department (Education) dated 12 April, 1873. It should, however, be noted that, although Bengali was introduced as a medium of instruction in the government sponsored schools, Assamese was retained in the missionary schools started in 1838. The American Baptist Mission, in fact, brought out an Assamese monthly paper entitled *Orunodoi* 'devoted to religion, science and general intelligence' from January, 1846. This paper and the missionary schools opened up a new vista to the western scientific education and discourses to the Assamese mass. From this initial stage, if one follows the growth and development of geographic literature in Assamese, one can discern three phases. The first phase started from 1846, with the publication of the *Orunodoi* and it continued for about a century till 1939, when the medium of Matriculation examination remained English and geography remained an optional subject. This was followed by a short period of about two decades, when the medium became Assamese and geography was raised to a compulsory subject at Matriculation level (with a paper of 50 marks from 1940 to 1950 and that of 100 marks from 1951 to 1975). Besides, this was also the period (from 1949) when geography was introduced at college level in Assam. These curricular changes necessarily resulted in writing higher level textbooks and carrying out discourses on various geographic aspects in Assamese. This, in its turn, facilitated the dawn of the third phase since about 1962, when efforts began to be made to publish geographic articles in Assamese science journals on the one hand, and coin relevant terminology in the language.

I

The publication of the *Orunodoi* from January, 1846 heralded the dawn of geographic literature in Assamese, *albeit* at an elementary level. In fact, the second issue of the *Orunodoi* (February 1846) brought out two articles, one on the solar system (*Grahar Dibaran*) and the other on the size of the earth (*Prithibir Akarar Bishoi*). The first article was an illustrated one with the relative positions of seven planets (Neptune and Pluto missing) and their sizes. The second article was on the discovery of America and spherical shape of the earth, which was substantiated with proofs. Starting with these the paper consistently brought out articles on general geography, dealing with physical and regional aspects separately. During the first year of its publication the paper published as many as seven articles covering geographical description of the northern hemisphere, Bhutan, Egypt, the Cape route, etc. Besides, some of these were devoted to economic aspects, such as iron ore as a resource and physical aspects eg. as to how rainfall is caused.

In the second year of publication, the *Orunodoi* continued to unveil the geographic facts, phenomena and events scientifically to the Assamese readers as before. Human geography was brought in by then with regional geography of Europe and the way of life of the American Indians, Chinese and Pacific islanders. This volume also introduced an ethnographic study of the Garos near home.

The third year issues in 1848 had six articles on geographic themes that dealt with lunar eclipse, mineral resources of Russia, the countries and capitals of Europe, British colonies and their individual populations, etc. besides having ethnographic studies on Naga, Khamti, Singpho, Mishmi, Adi, Hill Miri and Nishis and their relation with the plainsmen.

In the fourth year of its publication, the *Orunodoi* brought out articles on the area and population of the countries of the world, including that of the Pacific Islands. Some of these issues also published articles from a book, named *Asomiya Lorar Mitra* (The Friend of Young Assam), authored by Anandaram Dhekial Phukan, containing geographic treatment of the countries of the world, including their political systems, economy, trade and commerce and customs and traditions of their peoples. The author amazingly analysed the spatial variation of the natural conditions and their impact on human life.

The *Orunodoi* continued to bring out geographic articles delving deeper and deeper into the subject's contents throughout the eighteen fifties, sixties and seventies until it went out of publication in 1882. An examination of the articles published in this magazine reveals that the discourses were meant not only for the school students, but also for general public, who were expected to imbibe a scientific geographic temperament. The *Orunodoi* did not normally publish the names of the authors and it can be surmised that these articles were compiled and translated from relevant English books and encyclopaedias. These included not only descriptions but also laws and theories of physical geography. Some of the articles even described with illustration common climatic instruments. Thus, the magazine established a viable tradition of geographic literature in Assamese.

While the *Orunodoi* continued to be published till 1882, some other Assamese magazines started being published by the local editors from 1872. Many of these were short-lived but these also brought out geographic articles occasionally. For example, Gunabhiram Baruah brought out *Asom Bandhu* (Friend of Assam) in 1885 which contained articles on climatology (*Bari bignan*) and Earthquake (*Bhumikampa*). In the following year (1886) another serious magazine *Mou* (the Bee) produced by an England educated engineer, Balinarayan Borah and edited by his brother Haranarayan Borah, was first published. In its first issue (December 1886) it discussed the shape of the earth citing even proofs for its 'spheroidal' shape. The second issue (January 1887) dealt with the motions of the earth, earth's crust, the heat zones, latitudes and longitudes and their functions, etc. While discussing about the epiro-genic movement, one article pointed out the way in which water bodies and landmasses are distributed on the surface of the earth. The fourth issue in an article dealt with landforms and their evolution, influence of topography on climate, besides the causes of genesis of mountains. Next to this magazine, there came out *Jonaki* (the Firefly) in 1889, which also bore an article on Earthquake and its useful influences.

While geographic literature began to grow through these magazines, a few textbooks of school level also came out during the last century. In fact, a book entitled *Bhugolar Sikshak* (The Teacher of Geography) came out as far back as 1809. It was authored by 'A Missionary'. This was followed by *Asamiya Lorar Mitra*, Vol. 3, mentioned above, which came out part by part in *Orunodoi* from 1849. Eliza Brown brought out the third Assamese geography book, entitled *Bhugolar Bibaran* (Geographic Description) in 1851. This was followed by *Bhugolar Beej* (Seeds of Geography, 1873) by Ambika Charan

Ghosh, *Asamiya Lorar Bhugol,* (Geography for Assamese students, 1879) by Hemchandra Baruah *Prakrit Bhugol* (Physical Geography, 1884) by Ishananda Bharali, *Bhugol Siksa* (Lessons of Geography, 1895) by Kanaklal Baruah, *Assamiya Lorar Bhugol* (Geography of Assamese students, 1895) by Panindra Nath Gogoi, *Asamiya Lorar Bhugol Path* (Geography Lessons for Assamese students, 1896) by Krishna Prasad Agarwala, *Bhugol Darpan* (Geographic Mirror) by Padmanath Gohain Baruah and *Prakrit Bhugol* (Physical Geography) by Lambodhar Datta. The last two books perhaps came out in the first decade of this century.

The seriousness with which the tradition of geographic literature was sought to be set up can be realised from the fact that the writers and editors coined many new terms in Assamese for geographical features, events and phenomena, hitherto unknown in Assamese language. These included among others the terminology for Auaora, China, coal, compass, crater, gulf, lava, Mediterranean sea, navigator, railway, tide, United States of America, etc. The tradition of terminology coining continued from the *Orunodoi* through other magazines like *Assam Bilasini, Assam Bandhu, Mau, Jonaki,* and others.

With the turn of the century when the number of people receiving western education increased, a few books with specific geographic themes began to come out. The important among them were *Akash Rahasya* (1915) by Satyanath Bora on astronomy and solar system, *Parahasalirpara Biswabrahmandaloi* (From Primary School to the Universe, 1930's) by Durgadhar Barkataki, *Prakriti Darpan* (The Mirror of Nature, 1939) and *Manab Sabhyata* (Human Civilization, 1942) both by Raghunath Chaudhury. Of these books, the one by Barkataki dealt with physical and human geography almost exhaustively.

II

The introduction of geography as a compulsory course at the Matriculation level in 1940 that also in the medium of mother tongue, posed a great challenge to the academic community for there were no vernacular books of the required level. Heramba Kanta Barpujari, a professor of history, came forward to write out a textbook, *Bhugol Prabeshika,* (Matriculation Geography) in the early nineteen forties with the help of the series of *School Geography* by Dudley Stamp. It was an onerous task and the book turned out to be exhaustive for the required level and popular among all. This was followed by *Prabesika Bhugol Path* (Lessons on Matriculation Geography) of Dulal Barthakur, a school teacher, published in 1946. About the same time (1940's) Harinarayan Dutta Baruah, an eminent educationist, brought out *Bhugol Prabesh* (Matriculation Geography). It was in the nineteen fifties that a series of textbooks, covering the whole school syllabi from class VII to the Matriculation level, were brought out by a professional geographer, viz. Hariprasana Das, in collaboration with Kalicharan Das, another geography teacher. These textbooks not only popularised geography among the common Assamese readers, but also opened up avenues for discourses on a higher level in Assamese.

Apart from the textbooks, there came out only a few books written for intellectual public on various geographic themes. However, a few that came out include *Prithivir Katha* (About the Earth, 1950) by Baikuntha Barbara which discusses the origin of the earth, life on earth and evolution of man. The second book brought out by Axom Xahitya Xabha in 1958 entitled, *Simantar Sambad* (News from the Frontier) provides an anthropological account of the then NEFA, now Arunachal Pradesh. Mohammad Taher, a geography teacher, authored the third book '*Yatayat Aru Parivahan*' (The Means of transport) portraying the evolution of various means of transport. During three years between 1960 and 1962 there came out four more books, viz., *Prithibir Nana Desh* (Countries of the World - 1960) by Bhaben Baruah with lucid geographical treatment of important countries of the world, *Noir Sadhu* (Tales of Rivers, 1961) by Biswanarayan Shastri, highlighting the origin and course of the rivers and their activities, *Avishkarar Kahini* (The Stories of Discoveries—1961) by H.P. Das, a geographer, describing the important geographical explorations and discoveries and *Prithivir Purani Katha* (Stories of Ancient Earth—1969), authored by Jawaharlal Nehru and translated by Anu Baruah, containing the origin of the earth, life on earth and evolution of man. Although almost all of these books were of popular level, they can be taken as the spadework for discourses of professional nature that were to follow in the next phase.

III

The third or the contemporary phase of geographic writings in Assamese may be said to have started from 1962, with the publication of *Bijnan Jeuti*, the Assamese journal of the Assam Science Society. The Society side by side brought out lists and books containing Assamese version of scientific terminology and this paved the path for expressing geographical ideas and concepts in Assamese. It is seen that a geographical article, though written by a non-geographer (Baruah, H.P., *Banpani aru Garakhahania*) on flood and bank erosion in Assam started appearing in the second issue and ran through the fourth issue. The journal carried about 13 articles covering mainly physical aspects of geography. By 1970, the University of Gauhati set up the committee to bring out college level books in Assamese. This was subsequently followed by Dibrugarh University. The Gauhati University committee also brought out a voluminous glossary of science terminology in Assamese which carried about 4200 geographic terms. Within about 20 years from 1970, the Gauhati University Committee brought out about 32 books, 9 of them of higher secondary level and 23 of the graduation level, which covered all the auspects of college geography, including practicals and quantitative methods. Dibrugarh University brought out 2 higher secondary and 2 degree level books. Besides these, about 15 college level textbooks, written by college teachers, were published by private publishers after the medium switch-over. All these contributed to the growth of geographic discourses in Assamese at a much higher level. This trend was augmented by the setting up of the North East India Geographical Society which hold annual conferences, seminars and Symposia regularly.

The geographic literature of some standard in Assamese which has developed only in the last 35 years can be divided into the following sub-disciplines:

1. Geographic Thought and Philosophy

Geography being a relatively new discipline in the higher academic level, there has been still doubt among the public about its mooring and efficacy, therefore, several articles are devoted to consolidate the position of geography as a subject of intellectual and utilitarian import and make public realise that it no longer deals with 'where' and `what is where' alone, but also probes more important themes relating to man, environment and spatial differentiation. Bhagabati (1992), Bora (1992-93) and Bhagabati (again in 1998) lucidly deliberated upon changing philosophy and content of geography, its relationship with socio-economic development and environmental protection. The decision of the Board of Secondary Education, Assam, to replace geography by Social Studies (in 1973) at School Leaving Certificate Examination Level has disturbed the academic circle, for they are afraid of its dire consequences on the basic knowledge of the future generation. Deka (1988), Sarma (1992-93) and Das (1995) published articles against this decision with forceful arguments. Apart from dealing with the above preoccupations, there have come out deliberations on growing epistemic plurality in geography as can be seen in the writings of Bhagabati (1979), Sharma (1986), Taher (1986), Gogoi (1991 and 1993) and several others. Some writers again, are found to study the development and growth of geographic thought as reflected in the articles of Das (1988), Talukdar (1989-90 and 1996), Gogoi (1992-93) and Taher (1998).

2. Methodology and Cartographic Technique

As methods and techniques of analysis and interpretation of geographic facts and data are an unavoidable part of the subject, some writers have devoted to this aspect also. While Das (1986), Kar (1988), Sarma (1994) and Kar (1996) deal 'with various quantitative methods of data analysis, Bhagabati (1981) introduces the application of the principle of gravity model, and Borah (1989-90) and Kar (1995) explain the growing importance of remote sensing to area studies. Kar (1996) further discusses the growing use of computer technology, including digital cartography, G.I.S. and automated cartography and mapping and other visual expressions of geographic data analysis. A few others, including Talukdar (1989-90, 1995 and 1995-96) and Das (1991) lucidly deal with the history of development of cartography. Bhagabati (*Saphura*, Vol. 5 and Vol. 9, 1992) initiated a new series of discussion on the study of local geography through conscious observation.

3. General Geographic Themes

Origin and history of the earth, geographic treatment of some regions, countries, continents and oceans, and themes related to oceanography have found a wide reading. Gayan (1964), Borgohain (1978-79) and Sarma (1983) elaborately deal with the origin of the earth. Borgohain lucidly describes the Big Bang Theory of the origin of the Universe. Goswami (1969, 1972, 1973 and 1974) does a commendable job by translating *Gamow* on the origin and history of the earth. It is interesting to note that there have come out several articles on the origin, bottom configuration, resources and life in the oceans. Prominent among them are the writings of Bhagabati (1985-86, 1986 and 1992) and Das (1998) which highlight the bottom configuration, resources and strategic importance of the oceans. As for regional treatment, Bhattacharyya (1974), Barman (1983) and Phukan's (1992) analysis of the Antarctica and Bhagabati's (1983) Tundra provide interesting reading. Besides, there are regional analyses by Bhagabati (1986 and 1986) of Iran and Iraq, Das (1987) of Majuli island, Saikia (1995) of Goalpara and Taher (1997) of Lakhimpur, which turn out to be in-depth studies.

4. Geomorphology

North-East India is geomorphologically an interesting region for many reasons. It not only largely supports the Brahmaputra drainage system, but also is an area having Pre-Cambrian, Himalayan and Indo-Gangetic-Brahmaputra structures mixed up closely. Several papers therefore, are found to be devoted to the local geomorphology. In fact, floods and erosion caused by the Brahmaputra and its tributaries have become a pre-occupation of a large number of researches.

Baruah (1962 in two issues), Barman (1986), Das (1991), Goswami (1992), Borah (1995), Taher (1997) and Borah again (1998) deal with fluvial characteristics of the Brahmaputra and its tributaries, causes of flood and bank-erosion and measures needed to be taken to mitigate the devastating impact of these hazards. Some scholars are found to deal with numerous 'beels' or swamps, and ox-bow lakes that abound the limited plains of the region. Under this broad theme, Patra (1991) deals with the locational aspects of these lakelets, while Barman (1996-97) and Boro (1996-96) study Kapla Beel and Depar Beel respectively, bringing out their present status under the interference of ever increasing population. Two articles, based on research, show the microgeomorphology of the middle Kapili basin (Saikia, 1986) and process of sedimentation, silting and scouring in the Jịa Bharali channel (Bora, 1990). Other articles deal with historical geomorphology (Sarma, 1989-90), characteristics of the earth crust, fluvial processes (Patra, 1994), glacial processes (Hazarika, 1994) and evolution of geomorphological features against temporal dimension (Saikia, 1995).

5. Climatology

Climatological deliberations are relatively few in Assamese. Barthakur (1962) introduces to the science readers the history and development of climatology. He also writes (1967) on the keen relationship between weather and agriculture with special reference to that in Assam. While Pegu (1977) discusses the elements and structure of the atmosphere in a general way, Sarma (1977-78) deals with the origin and distribution of cyclones on the earth with special reference to those in the Indian Ocean, which often affect our weather. Borah (1985) elaborates in a lucid manner, the use of weather satellites in forecasts, which have increasingly become perfect and useful to common people in India.

6. Historical and Political Geography

Historical geography has become popular in Assam in that many geographers and non-geographers, especially the historians and linguists, have been trying to reconstruct physical and socio-cultural milieu of this region in the past. Among the geographers, Sarma (1984) examines the socio-cultural evolution of Nagaon district, while Ahmed deals with iron and steel industry in ancient India (1991) cottage industry of ancient Assam (1994) and growth and expansion of railways in North East India. Taher has systematically dealt with the historical geography of Goalpara (1994), Kamrup (1995) and Darrang (1996-97) districts in the nineteenth century, when the foundation of modern Assam was laid. Similarly, Sut Baruah (1992-93) and Deka (1996-97) write detailed socio-economic backgrounds of Dhakuakhana region and Goalpara District.

Although North East India has great strategic and geopolitical importance, the political geographic aspects have escaped the attention of the geographers. The only important discourse on this theme is that of Bhattacharyya and Lahkar (1990), which tries to delve into the causes of insurgency in the region. Bhattacharyya (1989-90) also deals with the then divided Berlin city, which was at the vortex of East and West European Geo-politics. Hazarika (1992-93), while pointing out the growing regionalism the world over, pleads for increasing emphasis on the study of political geography.

7. Population and Social Geography

The plural composition of the society in North East India, with its colourful variety and associated problems, has drawn the attention of many scholars of the region, especially in the last one decade. Dutta (1986) analyses the socio-economic backwardness of the tea-tribes of Assam. Bhagabati (1987) examines the tribes of Assam in their geographical backdrop and finds that they mostly live in economically less productive areas. Sarma (1990) also examines the tribes of Assam from locational point of view. Lahkar (1988), as a part of his M.Phil. research, examines the livelihood pattern of the slum-dwellers of Guwahati and finds them only marginally employed. Sarma (1988) and Kalita (1994) provide ethnographic study of the Tai-Khamti and Karbi communities respectively. Barman (1994-95) in a lengthy article, systematically deals with the evolution of society and culture in Assam in the existing geographical environment. Bhattacharyya (1995) examines Vaishnab Satra institutions of Majuli and points out their waning influence in social transformation. Majumdar (1996-97) examines the process of formation of Assamese nationality and points out the necessity to review its regionalism that harms the body-politics of itself. Taher (1991) analyses evolution of religion and impact of geographical conditions on religious ethos and practices.

Immigration and very high population growth are the burning problems of the region. Das (1979, 80) discusses in detail the problem of immigration in Assam. Kar (1992-93 and 1995), in a series of articles, analyses the trend of growth and associated problems and socio-economic structure of the population of Assam. He further examines the growth pattern of population of the state in comparison to that of other states of India in the recent decades to assess the degree of growth in the former objectively.

8. Economic Geography

Approaches to the study of economic geography have shifted much from the traditional ones. However, in Assamese, it started with the study of resources in general, as can be seen in the works of Bhattacharjee (1967), who studies the mineral resources, Chaudhury (1970) and Barkataki (1973) and Barthakur (1977) who deal with marine resources and underground water. Das later (1982) goes a step further and introduces the concept of Ocean Thermal Energy Conversion (OTEC) to the Assamese readers. Ahmed (1987) discusses the mining methods in North East India in the ancient period. There is also an illustrated discourse on geo-thermal energy by Das (1982). There came out quite a number of articles on the resource potentiality of Assam, as found in the works of Barua (1973), Das (1976), Mahanta (1981), Taher (1990) and Phukan and Mahanta (1991). Specific items of resource potentiality have also been elaborately discussed by Hazarika (Rubber industry: 1986), Borah (Brahmaputra water resource: 1995), Pathak (water resource potentiality: 1998) and Das (Cement, 1987).

9. Agricultural Geography

Agricultural geography has attracted the attention of only a few scholars. Hannan (1969) describes the problems of suitable soil and adequate supply of water and manure for agriculture in India as a whole. Land-use in North East India attracted the attention of Barthakur (1987), Das (1991) and Sarma (1995), who write on abuse and under-use of land, as also lack of effort to develop land for adequate use. Bhagabati (1986) examines the distribution of jhum cultivation in North-East India and relates its socio-economic implications on the one hand, and environmental merits and demerits on the other. The main thrust in agricultural geography has been found to be laid on various problems. Das has been pointing out (1970, 1972, 1990 and 1992) through various journals and periodicals the structural, institutional, physical and socio-economic problems of agriculture in Assam. Bhagabati (1992 and 1992) also has, through detailed study in smaller regions, mentioned about the problems of small farms and the potentiality they hold out, once the problems are addressed.

10. Settlement Geography

Settlement geography is an area, which has also escaped the attention of geographers in Assam. There have come out only a few articles in the themes under it, and those also deal only with urban geography, Bhagabati (1979-80) discusses the trend of urbanisation in Assam till 1971. He has also (1982) discussed the climate of the cities as tampered by man with his industrial, residential and transport activities intensified in such locations. Bhagabati (1986) further describes the evolution of Tezpur town since prehistoric period. Borah (1993), who visited China and made an excursion to the Peking Man Site at Dragon Bone Hill in Zhoukoudian in northern China, describes the habitat and the studies carried out there since 1921.

11. Biogeography

Like settlement geography, biogeography also has not received due coverage in Assamese. Das (1969) deals with ecology of the forests of Assam and classifies the major plant species that abound the forests and finally shows their distribution with maps. Sarma (1972) gives a vivid account of the ecology of the deserts and describes the animal life therein. Baishya (1983) deals with the life in Antarctica. The primate life, in which North East India is very rich, finds a systematic study in the discourse of Chaudhury, Tr. by Devi (1990), where the status of monkeys in Assam with special reference to Slow Loris, Pig tailed Macaque, Capped Langur, Hoolock Gibbon and such other endangered varieties.

12. Medical Geography

Medical geography is perhaps the least discussed geographical theme in Assamese. Only one article by M. Gopal Singh (1991), dealing with the causes and geographic locations of some diseases could be found. This article, however, attempts to show the influence of geographic factors on the occurrence of various diseases.

13.. Regional Development and Planning

Regional development and planning is a new introduction to geography that has come to its ambit following paradigmatic shift of geography in the recent past. However, it has gained popularity among the Indian geographers for obvious reasons. The techniques of planning, which have to be geo-economic, are often discussed in the journals and papers of Assam. Bhattacharyya (1971) employing geographical criteria divides North East India into planning regions. He also (in 3 issues in 1975) discusses the economy of Mizoram, which he argues as a glaring example of regional economic disparity; Bhagabati (1988) stresses the necessity of geographic study in understanding regional economic imbalance. Das (1996-96) casts thoughts on sustainable development aimed at eco-friendly planning of land use.

14. Geography of Environment

Like development and planning, geography of environment, embodying new approach of study, is a new introduction. The sub-discipline is found to be discussed from several points of view. Pathak (1979-80) discusses the influence of climate on civilization. Kalita (1984) comes down to a more practical field while pointing out the influence of climate on housetype. In an illustrated article he even shows the degree of slope of the roofs in relation to the speed of the prevailing wind. Chaudhury (1986) discusses the influence of forest on environment. Patra (1987) and Barman (1990) clearly show the impact of environment on life. On the other hand, a few writers have highlighted the effects of human interference on environment. Bhattacharyya (1979-80) discusses the impact of immigrant settlement on the flood-plains of the Brahmaputra valley and Sarma (1985) points out the deteriorating status of environment due to growing number and impact of human population. Environmental pollution and its impact have been deliberated on by Bora (1985), Bora (1987) and Goswami (1990). Goswami (1980) elaborately discusses the phenomenon of green house effect. Taher (1989-90) in an illustrated discourse describes the concept of eco-system, while Bhattacharyya (1996-97) deals with the potentiality of eco-tourism in Assam.

Conclusion

Geographic literature in Assamese is yet in its infancy. Apart from some textbooks and a few stray books by free-lance writers, no serious work on geographic themes came out till 1962. The medium imbroglio and non-inclusion of Geography as a compulsory subject in the high school final examination level till 1939 deterred and delayed the growth of geographic literature to a great extent.

The *Bhougolika* and the *Bijnan Jeuti*, the Assamese journals of North East India Geographical Society and Assam Science Society respectively, apart from the local magazines and papers, have helped the growth of geographic literature in Assamese. Although a large number of articles have so far come out, only a few books (other than textbooks) based on specific geographic themes, authored or edited, have seen the light of the day.

A sub-disciplinewise examination of the available literature shows that while the number of discourses is more in each of Geographic thought and philosophy, general geography, geomorphology, population and social geography, economic geography and geography and environment, it is few and far between in case of climatology, agricultural geography, settlement geography, biogeography and regional development and planning. Medical geography has been found to have discussed only once. This transpires a lesser degree of deliberations in the relatively new sub-disciplines, except Geography of Environment, which has caught the imagination of the geographers in the last one decade.

As for the qualitative aspect, while some of the discourses are of preliminary nature, quite a few reveal in-depth study and deep insight of the writers. The methodology employed in the works has been found to be satisfactory in many cases, but not so in their presentation, as can be seen from a large number of articles coming out without even requisite cartographic support.

The deliberations on the application of new techniques like remote sensing, digital cartography, GIS, etc. have been introduced. Similarly, discussions on epistemological plurality and paradigm - shift have also found place in Assamese. Apart from these, what is necessary is a social commitment to make geography yield benefit. If geography is to serve the society holistically, geographers of Assam must view the burning problems of the region, such as unusual growth of population, lingering ethnic troubles, frequent natural hazards, rapid destruction of environment, geographic isolation etc. and must now determine priorities. Such a concerted effort and purposeful theoretical basis alone will result in a positive feedback in, and enrichment of, geographic literature in Assamese.

BIBLIOGRAPHY

A. Articles

1. Geographic Thought and Philosophy

1. Bhagabati, A.K., 'Landscape: Bhugolbijnanar Eti Bitarkamulak Sabda' (Landscape: A Debateable Term in Geography), *Bijnan Jeuti*, Vol. 15, No. 2, 1979.
2. Sharma, H.N., 'Bhugolbijnanar Bartaman Paristhiti' (Present Status of Geography), *Bhougolika*, Vol. I, 1986.
3. Taher, M., 'Bhugolbijnanar Prakriti aru Darshan' (Nature and Philosophy of Geography), *Bhougolika*, Vol. I, 1986.
4. Mahanta, Prafulla, 'Bijnan, Bhugolbijnan aru Bijnanar darshan' (Science, Geography and Philosophy of Science), *Souvenir, 11th Conference, NEIGS*, Mariani College, 1986.
5. Das, Manmohan, 'Bhougolik Chinta-Charchar Krama-vikash' (Evolution of Geographic Thinking), *Bhougolika*, Vol. 3, 1988.
6. Deka, P., 'School Pathyakramat Bhugolbijnan' (The Place of Geography in School Syllabus), *Bhougolika*, Vol. 3, 1988.
7. Talukdar, S., 'Prachin Bharatiya Bijnan Charchat Prithivi Samparkiya Dharana' (Concepts Relating to the Earth in Ancient Indian Science), *Bhougolika*, Vol. 4, 1989–90.
8. Das, Manmohan, 'Bhugolbijnan Adhyayanat Paryabeshanar Gurutwa' (Importance of Observation in Geographical Studies), *Bhougolika*, Vol. 5, 1990.
9. Gogoi, Bhuban, 'Paribesh Bibhranti aru Bhougolik Darshanar Samparkar Bivached' (Environmental Confusion and a Watershed in the Geographic Philosophy), *Bhougolika*, Vol. 6, 1991.
10. Bhagabati, A.K., 'Bhugolatno Ami Ki Parho' (What Do We Stúdy in Geography), *Sophura*, No. 3, 1992.
11. Sarma, R., 'Bhougolik Manasikata aru Bhugol Siksha' (Geographic Temperament and Geography Education), *Bhougolika*, Vol. 7, 1992–93.
12. Gogoi, Bhuban, 'Bhougolik Nirnaybad: Bhugolar Eti Bishmitaprai Adhyay' (Geographic Determinism: A Forgotten Chapter of Geography), *Bhougolika*, Vol. 7, 1992–93.
13. Borah, A.K., 'Bhugol Sikshar Prayojaniyata' (Necessity of Geography Education), Sandhan, *Journal of the Tezpur Sub-Divisional Middle School Teachers' Association*, Vol. 11, No. 6, 1992–93.
14. Patra, J.K., 'Bhugol Bijnan, Adhyan, Adhyapana' (Geography: Teaching and Learning), *Bhougolika*, Vol. 9, 1995.
15. Das, M., 'Sampratik Asomat Bhugol Adhyayanar Prasangikata' (Relevance of Geography Education in the Present Day Assam), *Souvenir, 18th Conference, NEIGS*, Goalpara College, 1995.
16. Talukdar, S., 'Aprameya Tolemy aru Teonr Anwasha' (Ptolemy, the Depthless Scholar and His Search), *Bhougolika*, Vol. 10, 1995–96.
17. Bhagabati, A.K., 'Bhugol Sikshar Mahatwa' (The Importance of Geography Education), *Souvenir, 1st Session of All Assam Geographical Society*, Pathsala, 1996.

18. Taher, M., 'Anchal aru Anchalik Bhugol' (Region and Regional Geography), *Souvenir, 20th Conference, NEIGS*, Nowgong College, 1998.

2. Methodology and Cartographic Techniques

1. Bhagabati, A.K., 'Bhugol Bijnanat Abhikarsh Adarsha' (Gravity Model in Geography), *Bijnan Jeuti*, Vol. 16, No. 2, 1981.
2. Das, M., 'Bhugol Bijnan aru Eyar Adhyayanar Paddhati' (Geography and Its Methodology), *Bhougolika*, Vol. 1, 1986.
3. Chaharia, C., 'Prithivir Manchitra Ankan' (Technique of Drawing Map of the Earth), *Bhougolika*, Vol. 2, 1987.
4. Kar, B., 'Akshangsha, Draghimansha aru Manchitra Abhikshep' (Latitude, longitude and Map Projection), *Bhougolika*, Vol. 3, 1988.
5. Borah, P., 'Bhougolik Adhyayanat Sudu-Sangbedan Paddhatir Prayog' (Application of Remote Sensing in Geographical Studies), *Bhougolika*, Vol. 4, 1989–90.
6. Das, M., 'Prithivir Manchitra Ankanar Paddhati aru Itihas' (Cartography and Its History), *Ajir Asom*, Nov. 17, 1991.
7. Bhagabati, A.K., 'Gaonar Bhugol' (Village/Local Geography), *Saphura*, Vol. 5, 1992.
8. Bhagabati, A.K., 'Schoolaloi Jaote Bhugol' (Geographical Observation While Going to School), *Saphura*, Vol. 9, 1992.
9. Sarma, S., 'Manchitra Ankanar Eti Chamu Bivaran' (A Short Account of Map Drawing), *Bhougolika*, Vol. 8, 1994.
10. Bhattacharyya, P., 'Asamot Manchitrar Parampara' (Tradition of map Drawing in Assam), *Bhougolika*, Vol. 8, 1994.
11. Talukdar, S., 'Prachin Bharatiya Manchitra Bidya' (Cartography of Ancient India), *Bhougolika*, Vol. 9, 1995.
12. Saikia, L., 'Manchitra: Janasanjugar Anya Ek Madhyam' (Map: A Medium of Mass Communication), *Bhougolika*, Vol. 9, 1995.
13. Kar, B., 'Dur-Sangbedan aru Bhougolik Adhyayanat Eyar Prayog' (Remote Sensing and its Application in Geographic Studies), *Souvenir, 18th Conference, NEIGS*, Goalpara College, 1995.
14. Kar, B., 'Bhougolik Taithya Bisleshan Pranali' (Methods of Analysing Geographic Data), *Bijnan Jeuti*, Vol. 30, No. 6, 1996.

3. General Geographic Themes

1. Gayan, H., 'Prithibir Adi Itihas' (Early History of the Earth), *Bijnan Jeuti*, Vol. 2, No. 2, 1964.
2. Gamow, G. Tr.; Goswami, D.C., 'Prithibi Namar Grahato' (The Planet, Called Earth), *Bijnan Jeuti*, Vol. 5, No. 2, 1969.
3. Barthakur, Kabita, 'Abhishapta Bhubhag' (The Cursed Region), *Bijnan Jeuti*, Vol. 7, No. 4, 1971.
4. Das, M., 'Asomar Arthanaitik Unnayanat Bhougolik Avasthanar Prabhav' (Influence of Location on the Economic Development of Assam), *Payobhora*, 1972.
5. Gamow, G., Tr.; Goswam, D.C., 'Weizeckerar Theory' (Weizecker's Theory), *Bijnan Jeuti*, Vol. 8, No. 3, 1972.

6. Das, M., 'Bhougolik Dristit Kamrup Jila' (Kamrup District from Geographical Perspective), *Payobhara*, 1973.
7. Gamow, G., Tr.; Goswam, D.C., 'Amar Biswasi Jonti' Our Dependable Moon), *Bijnan Jeuti*, Vol. 9, No. 2, 1973.
8. Bhattacharyya, N.N., 'Antarctikiya Himstupar Talar Hrad' (The Lakes under the Antarctic Ice Caps), *Bijnan Jeuti*, Vol. 10, No. 1, 1974.
9. Goswami, D.C., 'Bilopta Mahadesh Atlantic' (The Drowned Continent, Atlantis), *Bijnan Jeuti*, H.C. Bhuyan Memorial Volume, Assam Science Society, 1974.
10. Goswami, D.C., "Ekhan Prithivi, Bahut Akriti' (One Earth, Many Shapes), *Bijnan Jeuti*, Vol. 2, No. 1, 1975.
11. Borgohain, P., 'Biswabrahmandar Shristi: Big Bang' (The Origin of the Universe: Big Bang), *Bijnan Jeuti*, Vol. 15, No. 4, 1978–79.
12. Das, M., 'Pustikar Khadya aru Eyar Bitaranat Bhougolik Boishamya' (Nutritious Food and Geographic Disparity in Its Distribution), *Bijnan Jeuti*, Vol. 17, No. 4, 1982.
13. Barman, R., 'Kumeru Mahadeshar Eti Bhougolik Bivaran' (A Geographical Description of Antarctic Continent), *Bijnan Jeuti*, Vol. 18, No. 2, 1983.
14. Bhagabati, A.K., 'Tundra Anchalar Jalbayu, Udbhid aru Jivajantu' (The Climate, Vegetation and Animals of Tundra), *Bijnan Jeuti*, Vol. 18, No. 4, 1983.
15. Sarma, S., 'Biswabrahmandar Bisaye Dui Eta Katha' (A Few Facts about the Universe), *Bijnan Jeuti*, Vol. 18, No. 6 and 7, 1983.
16. Bhagabati, A.K., 'Uttal Samudrar Katha' (Facts about the Restless Ocean), *Bijnan Jeuti*, Vol. 20, No. 5, Vol. 21, No. 1, 1985–86.
17. Bhagabati, A.K., 'Iran' (Iran), *Bijnan Jeuti*, Vol. 21, No. 2, 1986.
18. Bhagabati, A.K., 'Iraq' (Iraq), *Bijnan Jeuti*, Vol. 21, No. 4, 1986.
19. Bhagabati, A.K., 'Mahasagar aru Ami' (We and the Ocean), *Prantic*, Vol. 5, No. 19, 1986.
20. Das, M., 'Majuli: Eti Bhougalik Samiksha' (Majuli: A geographical Treatment), *Ajir Asom*, Aug. 30, 1987.
21. Bhagabati, A.K., 'Bharatar Kasharia Sagar Mahasagar' (The Neighbouring Seas and Ocean of India), *Bijnan Jeuti*, Vol. 27, No. 1, 1992.
22. Phukan, D., 'Antarctica, Bhabishyatar Biwa Udyan' (Antarctica, the Future park of the Earth), *Bijnan Jeuti*, Vol. 27, No. 1, 1992.
23. Mahanta, A.P., 'Bharatar Udbhidmondal: Ek Bhougolik Paryyalocana' (The Vegetation of India: A Geographical Review), *Bhougolika*, Vol. 7, 1992–93.
24. Saikia, A.R., 'Goalpara Jilar Bhugol' (Geography of Goalpara District), *Souvenir, 18th Conference, NEIGS*, Goalpara College, 1995.
25. Taher, M., 'Lakhimpur, Awasthiti aru Sambhavana' (Lakhimpur, Geographical Status and Potentiality), *Swarnashree, Souvenir of the Silver Jubilee Celebration of Lakhimpur District*, 1997.
26. Gogoi, Rajiv, 'Tushar Yug: Mrityur Ek Sital Shiharan' (Glacial Period: A Cold Touch of Death), *Bijnan Jeuti*, Vol. 32, No. 4, 1997–98.
27. Chetia, B., 'Matir Talar Pani' (Underground Water), *Bijnan Jeuti*, Vol. 32, No. 4, 1997–98.
28. Das, P.K., 'Sagarar Alankar' (Ornament of the Ocean: The Coral), *Bijnan Jeuti*, Vol. 32, No. 5, 1998.

29. Bhattacharyya, N.N., 'Ushna Prithibi aru Utthita Samudrapristha' (The Warm Earth and the Rising Ocean Bed), *Bijnan Jeuti*, Vol. 32, No. 6, 1998.

4. Geomorphology

1. Baruah, H.P., 'Banpani aru Garakhahnia' (Flood and bank Erosion), *Bijnan Jeuti*, Vol. 1, No. 2, 1962.
2. Bhattacharyya, N.N., 'Thar Marubhumit Ebhumuki' (A Glimpse of the Thar Desert), *Bijnan Jeuti*, Vol. 1, No. 3, 1962.
3. Chaudhury, J.M., 'Prithibir Utpatti aru Gathan' (The Origin and Structure of the Earth), *Bijnan Jeuti*, Vol. 1, No. 3, 1962.
4. Gayan, H.K., 'Prithivir Kholato' (The Crust of the Earth), *Bijnan Jeuti*, Vol. 1, No. 4, 1962.
5. Sarma, P.K., 'Chalanshil Bharat' (The Moving Indian Landmass), *Bijnan Jeuti*, Vol. 19, No. 5, 1984.
6. Barman, R., 'Brahmaputra Nadi aru Eyar Upatyaka: Eti Bhougolik Sameeksha' (The River Brahmaputra and its Valley: A Geographical Discussion), *Bhougolika*, Vol. 1, 1986.
7. Saikia, R., 'Kapilir Pare Pare' (Along the Bank of Kapili), *Bhougolika, Vol. 2, 1986.*
8. Sarma, J.K., 'Saharato Edin Achil Himbahar Sitalata' (Sahara Once Had the Cold of Glacier), *Bhougolika*, Vol. 4, 1989–90.
9. Hazarika, P.K., 'Baraph aru Baraphar Noi' (Snow and Glacier), *Bijnan Jeuti*, Vol. 25, No. 1, 1990.
10. Borah, A.K., 'Nadi-Garbhar Prakriyasamuhar Swarup' (The Processes in a River), *Bhougolika*, Vol. 5, 1990.
11. Das, U.C., 'Asomar Banpani Samasya aru Eyar Pratikar' (The Flood Problem in Assam and Its Remedy), *Bhougolika*, Vol. 6, 1991.
12. Patra, J.K., 'Asomar Beelar Paristhitik Bhugol' (Location and Status of the 'Beels' of Assam), *Bhougolika*, Vol. 6, 1991.
13. Goswami, D.C., 'Brahmaputra aru Eyar Avavahika Anchalar Parivesh' (The Environment of the Brahmaputra and Its Basin Area), *Bijnan Jeuti*, Vol. 27, No. 1, 1992.
14. Patra, J.K., 'Noir Pani Bagare Koloi' (Where Does the River Water Roll Down to?), *Bhougolika*, Vol. 8, 1994.
15. Saikia, R., 'Bhu-Prakritik Bijnan aru Samay' (Geomorphology and Time), *Bhougolika*, Vol. 9, 1995.
16. Borah, A.K., 'Asomar Ban: Dhwangsha aru Parimapar Samashya' (Floods in Assam: Destruction and Problem of Assessment), *Ajir Asom*, August 20, 1995.
17. Barman, P.C., 'Kapla Beelar Atit aru Bartaman' (The Present and Future of the Kapla Beel), *Bhougolika*, Vol. 10, 1996–97.
18. Boro, G., 'Deepar Beel, Sangrakshan aru Samasya' (Deepar Beel: Problems of Conservation), *Bhougolika*, Vol. 10, 1996–97.
19. Taher, M., 'Brahmaputra: Eti Bhougolik Parichiti' (The Brahmaputra: A Geographical Introduction), *Bijnan Jeuti*, Vol. 32, No. 1, 1997.
20. Borah, A.K., 'Brahmaputrar Ban Niyantran' (Control of Floods of the Brahmaputra), *Amar Asom*, Sept. 9, 1998.

5. Climatology

1. Barthakur, M., 'Batar Bijnanar Itihas' (History of Climatology), *Bijnan Jeuti*, Vol. 1, No. 2, 1962.
2. Barthakur, M., 'Batar or Krishi' (Weather and Agriculture), *Bijnan Jeuti*, Vol. 3, No. 4, 1967.
3. Pegu, Puwalmani, 'Bayur gathan' (Structure of the Atmosphere), *Bijnan Jeuti*, Vol. 13, No. 2, 1977.
4. Pegu, Puwalmani, 'Bayumandal' (The Atmosphere), *Bijnan Jeuti*, Vol. 13, No. 3, 1977.
5. Sarma, S., 'Ba-Marali' (Cyclone), *Bijnan Jeuti*, Vol. 13, No. 5, 1977–78.
6. Borah, L., 'Batarar Purbavas' (Weather Forecasting), *Bijnan Jeuti*, Vol. 20, No. 4, 1985.

6. Historical and Political Geography

1. Sarmah, P.K., 'Aitiyyamandit Nagaon Jila' (The Glorious Nagaon District), *Souvenir, 9th Conference, NEIGS*, Nagaon, 1984.
2. Bhattacharyya, N.N., 'Berlin Sahar aru Pub-Europiya Bhu-Rajniti' (The City of Berlin and East European geo-Plitics), *Bhougolika*, Vol. 4, 1989–90.
3. Bhattacharyya, N.N. and Lahkar, B., 'Uttar-Pub Bharatar Sampratik Raj-Biplavar Eti Bhougolik Alochana' (A Geographical Discussion on the Current Political Unrest in North-East India), *Bhougolika*, Vol. 5, 1990.
4. Ahmed, P., 'Prachin Bharatar Lo-Tikhar Silpa' (Iron and Ancient History of Ancient India), *Bhougolika*, Vol. 6, 1991.
5. Hazarika, J.S., 'Bhu-rajnitir Punar Mulyankan' (Re-evaluation of Geo-Politics), *Bhougolika*, Vol. 7, 1992–93.
6. Sut Baruah, S., 'Bhougolik Dristibhangit Dhakuakhanar Aitihasik Paristhiti' (Historical Geography of Dhakuakhana), *Bhougolika*, Vol. 7, 1992–93.
7. Taher, M., 'Unabingsha Satikar Goalpara: Aitihasik Bhugolar Ekhila Pat' (Goalpara District in the Nineteenth Century: A Leaf from Historical Geography), *Bhougolika*, Vol. 8, 1994.
8. Ahmed, P., 'Prachin Asamar Kutir Silpa' (Cottage Industry of Ancient Assam), *Bhougolika*, Vol. 8, 1994.
9. Taher, M., 'Unabingsha Satikar Kamrup: Aitihasik Bhugolar Ekhila Pat' (Kamrup District in the Nineteenth Century: A Leaf from Historical Geography), *Bhougolika*, Vol. 9, 1995.
10. Ahmed, P., 'Uttar-Pub Bharat Rail Path Pravartan aru Samprasaran' (Establishment and Expansion of Railways in North-East India), *Bhougolika*, Vol. 9, 1995.
11. Taher, M., 'Unabingsha Satikar Darrang: Aitihasik Bhugolar Ekhila Pat' (Darrang District in the Nineteenth Century: A Leaf from Historical Geography), *Bhougolika*, Vol. 10, 1996–97.
12. Deka, S. P., 'Aitihasik Dristire Goalpara Jilar Bhugol' (Geography of Goalpara District from Historical View Point), *Bhougolika*, Vol. 10, 1996–97.

7. Population and Social Geography

1. Das, H.P., 'Asamot Anupraveshar Samasya' (Problem of Immigration in Assam), *Bijnan Jeuti*, Vol. 15, No. 2, 1979–80.
2. Dutta, M.L., 'Asamor Chah-Jangosthir Artha-Samajik Anagrasarata' (The Socio-Economic Backwardness of the Tea Tribes of Assam), *Bhougolika*, Vol. 1, 1986.
3. Bhagabati, A.K., 'Bhougolik Chitrapatat Asomar Janajati' (The Tribes of Assam in the Geographical Backdrop), *Sonitprabha*, Tezpur Branch of Axom Xahitya Xabha, 1987.
4. Lahkar, B., 'Guwahati Mahanagarir Bastibasisakalar Jivika' (The Livelihood Pattern of the Slum Dwellers of Guwahati City), *Bhougolika*, Vol. 3, 1988.
5. Sarma, K., 'Asomar Tai-Khamti Janagosthi' (The Tai-Khamti Community of Asam), *Bhougolika*, Vol. 3, 1988.
6. Das, M., 'Asomar Janajatiya Samasya: Andolan and Samadhan' (Tribal Problem of Assam: Agitation and Solution), *Ninad*, 1989.
7. Sarma, R., 'Bhougolik Dristikonarpara Asomar Janajatiya Samasya aru Eyar Samadhanar Upay' (Problems of the Tribes of Assam and their Solution from Geographical Viewpoint), *Bhougolika*, Vol. 5, 1990.
8. Taher, M., 'Dharma aru Bhugol' (Religion and Geography), *Souvenir, 15th Conference, NEIGS*, Tihu College, 1991.
9. Kar, B., 'Uttar-Pub Bharatar Janasankhya Briddhir Swarup' (Pattern of Population Growth in North-East India), *Bhougolika*, Vol. 7, 1992–93.
10. Bhuyan, J.C., 'Jana-Bishfuran aru Paribeshar Awanati' (Population Explosion and Deterioration of Environment), *Bijnan Jeuti*, Vol. 29, No. 1, 1994.
11. Kalita, B., 'Karbi Anglong aru Karbi Samaj' (Karbi Anglong and Karbi Society), *Bhougolika*, Vol. 8, 1994.
12. Barman, R., 'Bhougolik Paribeshat Asomar Samaj aru Sanskriti: Eti Paddhatigata Alochana' (Society and Culture of Assam in Its Geographical Environment: A Systematic Study), *Axom Xahitya Xabha Patrika*, Vol. 50, No. 3, 1994–95.
13. Kar, B., 'Asomar Janasankhyar Swarup' (Population Characteristics of Assam), *Bhougolika*, Vol. 9, 1995.
14. Kar. B., 'Asomar Janasankhya Briddhi aru Tatjanit Samasya' (Population Growth in Assam and Resultant Problems), *Asom bani*, March 24, 1995.
15. Bhattacharyya, N.N., 'Barluitar Bukur Suwani Majuli' (The Beautiful Majuli Island on the Brahmaputra), *Asom Bani*, June 2, 1995.
16. Kar. B., 'Asomar Janasankhya Briddhi Aswabhavik Haicheneki' (Is the Population Growth in Assam Unnatural), *Asom bani*, Sept. 2, 1995.
17. Majumdar, P., 'Jati, Jatiyatabad aru Asomiya Jati (Nationality, nationalism and Assamese Nationality), *Bhougolika*, Vol. 10, 1996–97.

8. Economic geography (Resource, Industry, etc.)

1. Bhattacharjee, C.C., 'Khanij Sampad' (Mineral Resources), *Bijnana Jeuti*, Vol. 3, No. 3, 1967.

2. Choudhury, P.K., 'Sagartalir Sampadar Katha' (Resources of the Sea Floor), *Bijnana Jeuti*, Vol. 6, No. 2, 1970.
3. Bhattacharyya, N.N., 'Bharatar Morapat Silpar samasya' (Problems of the Indian Jute Industry), *Payobhara*, Vol. 2, No. 26, 1972.
4. Barua, Kumari R., 'Asomar Prakritik Sampadsamuhar Boijnanik Prayog' (Scientific Utilisation of the natural Resources of Assam), *Bijnana Jeuti*, Vol.9, No. 3, 1973.
5. Barkataki, D., 'Sagarar Panir Amulya Sampad' (Invaluable Resources of the Sea), *Bijnana Jeuti*, Vol. 9, No. 4, 1973.
6. Das, L., 'Asomar Banaj Sampad' (Forest Resources of Assam), *Bijnana Jeuti*, Vol. 12, No. 3, 1976.
7. Barthakur, J.R., 'Bhu-Tal Jal: Utpatti, Aharan aru Byavahar' (Underground Water: Origin, Exploitation and Utilisation), *Bijnana Jeuti*, Vol. 13, No. 1, 1977.
8. Mahanta, P.K., 'Amar Banasampad aru Ami' (We and Our Forest Resources), *Bijnana Jeuti*, Vol. 16, No. 5 & 6, 1981.
9. Das, M., 'Sagararpara Sakti Aharan' (Tapping Energy from Ocean), *Bijnana Jeuti*, Vol. 17, No. 1, 1982.
10. Das, P.K., 'Bhu-Tap Sakti' (Geo-Thermal Energy), *Bijnana Jeuti*, Vol. 17, No. 13, 1982.
11. Hazarika, B., 'Asomat Rubber Udyog' (Rubber Industry in Assam), *Bijnana Jeuti*, Vol. 21, No. 5, 1986.
12. Ahmed, P., 'Prachin Kalat Uttar Pub Bharatat Khaniz Sampad Uddhar' (Extraction of Mineral in North East India in the Ancient Period), *Bhougolika*, Vol. 2, 1987.
13. Das, P.K., 'Bilati Mati, Sunsil aru Uttar-Purbanchal' (Cement, Limestone and the North Eastern Region), *Bijnana Jeuti*, Vol. 22, No. 2, 1987.
14. Taher, M., 'Asomar Prakritik Sampad' (Natural Resources of Assam), *Asomiya Rachana Sankalan*, Ed. Baruah, T., Students' Store, Guwahati, 1990.
15. Phukan, P. and Mahanta, P., 'Asomar Jalasampadar Lagat Samparkita Keitaman Katha' (A Few Points Related to the Water Resources of Assam), *Bhougolika*, Vol. 6, 1991.
16. Saikia, B., 'Asomar Arthanitit Chah Silpar Bhumika' (The Role of Tea Industry in the Economy of Assam), *Bhougolika*, Vol. 9, 1995.
17. Borah, A.K., 'Brahmaputrar Jalasampad: Unnayan Samasya Aru Sambhavana' (Water Resources of the Brahmaputra: Potentiality and Problem of Its Development), *Bhougolika*, Vol. 9, 1995.
18. Pathak, K., 'Brahmaputra, Jalasampadar Byavahar aru Prachuryya' (Utilisation and Abundance of Water Resources of the Brahmaputra), *Bijnana Jeuti*, Vol. 32, No. 6, 1998.

9. Agricultural Geography

1. Hannan, M.A., 'Bharatar Krishikarya, Mati, Pani, Sar Adir Samasya aru Tar Samadhan' (Problem of Soil, Water and Manure in the Agriculture of India and Its Solution), *Bijnana Jeuti*, Vol. 5, No. 1, 1969.

2. Das, M., 'Asomar Bhoiyamar Krishisamasya' (Problem of Agriculture in the Plains of Assam), *Saptahik Nilachal*, Sept. 23, 1970.
3. Bhagabati, A.K., 'Uttar Pub Bharatar Jhum Kheti' (Jhum Cultivation in North East India), *Souvenir, Special Session on Role of Science and Technology in Rural Development*, Assam Science Society, 1986.
4. Barthakur, M., 'Bhumi Byavahar aru Asomar Krishi Samasya' (Land-use and Agricultural Problems of Assam), *Bhougolika*, Vol. 2, 1987.
5. Das, M., 'Krishi Pariveshar Uparat Banpani Niyantran Byavasthar Prabhav' (Influence of the Flood Control Measures on Agricultural Environment), *Deuka*, No. 9, 1990.
6. Das, M., 'Asomar Bhumi Byavaharar Samasya (Problem of Land-use in Assam), *Bhougolika*, Vol. 6, 1991.
7. Bhagabati, A.K., 'Asamar Kshudra Krishi: Samasya aru Sambabhana' (Small-Scale Agriculture in Assam: Problem and Prospect), *Ajir Asom*, 1992.
8. Das, M., 'Asamor Krishi Samasya aru Eyar Samadhan' (Problem of Agriculture in Assam and Its Solution), *Deuka*, No. 1, 1992.
9. Bhagabati, A.K., 'Asamor Krishi Samasya aru Eyar Samadhan' (Problem of Agriculture in Assam and their Solution), *Deuka*, No. 7, 1992.
10. Sarma, Siddhinath, 'Goalpara Jilar Bhumi Byavahar' (Land-use of Goalpara District), *Souvenir, 18th Conference of NEIGS*, Goalpara College, 1995.

10. Settlement Geography

1. Bhagabati, A.K., 'Nagarikaran aru Asom' (Urbanisation and Assam), *Bijnan Jeuti*, Vol. 15, No. 5, 1979–80.
2. Bhagabati, A.K., 'Nagar Anchalar Jalbayu' (Climate of the Urban Areas), *Bijnan Jeuti*, Vol. 17, No. 1, 1982.
3. Bhagabati, A.K., 'Tezpur Nagari: Atit aru Bartaman' (Tezpur Town: Past and Present), *Souvenir, 35th Annual Session, Assam College Teachers Association*, Tezpur, 1986.
4. Borah, A.K., Peking Manabar Adim Abas' (The Early Habitat of Peking Man), *Prantik*, Vol. 12, No. 10, 1993.

11. Biography

1. Das, Niloy Kumar, 'Amar Udbhid aru Banabhumir Bisaye Eti Toka' (A Note on Our Plants and Forests), *Bijnan Jeuti*, Vol. 5, No. 4, 1969.
2. Sharma, Soneswar, 'Marubhumiloi Jao Bola' (Let us go to Desert), *Bijnan Jeuti*, Vol. 7, No. 2, 1972.
3. Baishya, Dinesh, 'Kumeru Mahadeshar Prani' (The Animal Life of Antarctica), *Bijnan Jeuti*, Vol. 18, No. 2, 1983.
4. Chaudhuri, A., (Tr. Devi, Rajlakshmi), 'Asomar Bandar: Eti Dristipat', *Bijnan Jeuti*, Vol. 25, No. 2, 1990.

12. Medical Geography

1. Singh, M. Gopal, 'Medical Bhugolat Rugar Karan aru Sthan Nirnay: Eti Chamu Alochana' (Identification of Causes and Places of Occurrence of Disease in Medical Geography), *Bhougolika*, Vol. 6, 1991.

13. Regional Development and Planning

1. Bhattacharyya, N.N., 'Uttar-Pub Bharatar Parikalpana Anchalsamuh' (The Planning Regions of North East India), *Payobhara*, Vol. 2, No. 16, 1971.
2. Bhattacharyya, N.N., 'Mizoram: Bhougolik Dristire Anchalik Baishamya Bichar' (Mizoram: An Appraisal of Regional Imbalance from Geographical Angle), *Payobhara*, Vol. 6, Nos. 1, 2, and 3, 1995.
3. Bhagabati, A.K., 'Anchalik Boishamya aru Bhaugolik Adhyayanar Tatparyya' (Regional Disparity and the Significance of Geographical Study), *Souvenir, 34th Annual Session, Assam Science Society*, 1988.
4. Das, Manmohan, 'Dharanksham Unnayan aru Amar Kartavya' (Sustainable Development and our Duty), *Bhougolika*, Vol. 10, 1996–97.

14. Geography of Environment

1. Bhattacharyya, N.N., 'Asomar Paristhitik Pariveshar Oparat Utpravasi Basatir Prabhav' (Impact of Immigrant Settlement on the Natural Environment of Assam), *Bijnan Jeuti*, Vol. 15, No. 5, 1979–80.
2. Pathak, Khanindra, 'Jalbayu, Sabhyata aru Ami' (Climate, Civilisation and We), *Bijnan Jeuti*, Vol. 15, No. 6, 1979–80.
3. Kalita, Gadadhar, 'Griha Nirmanar Oparat Vayumandalayar Prabhav' (Influence of Climate on House Construction), *Bijnan Jeuti*, Vol. 19, No. 6, 1984.
4. Sharma, Soneswar, 'Prakiritir Oporat Manuhar Prabhav' (Man's Impact on Nature), *Bijnan Jeuti*, Vol. 19, No. 2, 1985.
5. Pathak, Subhash, 'Banyaprani Sangrakshan: Prasanga Asom' (Conservation of Wild Life in the Context of Assam), *Bijnan Jeuti*, Vol. 20, No. 2, 1985.
6. Borah, Lalit Chandra, 'Parivesh Pradusan' (Environmental Pollution), *Bijnan Jeuti*, Vol. 20, No. 3, 1985.
7. Chaudhury, B., "Sustha Bhougolik Parivesh aru Aranya' (Sound Geographical Environment and Forest), *Bhougolika*, Vol. 1, 1986.
8. Bhattacharyya, N.N., 'Kaziranga Parivesh Nikay aru Aranya' (The Environment of Kaziranga and Forest), *Bhougolika*, Vol. 1, 1986.
9. Deka, Tarinicharan, 'Anavik Yugar Aranyat Sangrakshanar Dikshamantra' (Clue to Conservation of the Forests of the Atomic Age), *Bhougolika*, Vol. 2, 1987.
10. Patra, J.K., 'Pakshi-Padap Parivesh' (Avi-Fauna and Vegetation), *Bhougolika*, Vol. 2, 1987.
11. Borah, J., 'Brahmaputra Upatyakar Dushita Pariparshikata' (The Polluted Environment of Brahmaputra Valley), *Bhougolika*, Vol. 2, 1987.

12. Goswami, B.N., 'Green House Effect: Somayar Abhan' (Green House Effect: Call of the Time), *Bhougolika*, Vol. 3, 1988.
13. Taher, M., 'Parivesh aru Pariveshtantra' (Environment and Eco-System), *Bhougolika*, Vol. 4, 1989–90.
14. Khangiya, B., 'Produshan Niyantranat Brikhyaropanar Bhumika' (The Role of Afforestation in Controlling Environment), *Bhougolika*, Vol. 4, 1989–90.
15. Barman, R., 'Jivar Oporat Jalabayur Prabhab: Eti Bhougolik Alochana' (Influence of Climate on Life: A Geographical Discussion), *Bhougolika*, Vol. 5, 1990.
16. Goswami, B.N., 'Parivesh Sankat' (Environmental Crisis), *Bhougolika*, Vol. 5, 1990.
17. Barman, R., 'Manuhar Oporat Himakryar Prabhab' (Influence of Glaciation on Mankind), *Bhougolika*, Vol. 9, 1995.
18. Bhattacharyya, P., 'Paryatan, Paryatanar Bhugol aru Asom' (Tourism, Geography of Tourism and Assam), *Bhougolika*, Vol. 10, 1996–97.

B. Books

1. Barkataki, D., *Parhasalirpara Biswabrahmandaloi* (From primary School to the Universe), Barkataki and Co., Jorhat, 1936.
2. Choudhury, R., *Prakriti Darshan* (Mirror of Nature), Kamrup Prakash Bhavan, Patacharkuchi, 1939.
3. Barborah, B., *Prithivir Katha* (About the Earth), Orient Longman, Calcutta, 1950.
4. Chaliha, P.D. ed., *Simantar Sambad*, Assam Xahitya Xabha, Jorhat, 1958.
5. Taher, M., *yatayat aru Parivahan* (Transportation), Assam Publication Board, Guwahati, 1960.
6. Baruah, B., *Prithivir Nana Desh* (Countries of the World), Dutta Baruah & Co., Nalbari, 1960.
7. Shastri, B.N., *Noir Sadhu* (Stories about Rivers), Oriental Book Co., Guwahati, 1961.
8. Das, H.P., *Avishkarar Kahini* (Stories of Discoveries), Assam Publication Board, Guwahati, 1961.
9. Nehru, J. Tr. Baruah, A., *Prithivir Purani Katha* (Early Days of the Earth), Lawer's Book Stall, Guwahati, 1962.
10. Das, H.P., *Asomar Banaj Sampad* (Forest Resources of Assam), Assam Academi, Guwahati, 1964.
11. Shastry, B.N., *Himalay Katha* (Stories about the Himalaya), Oriental Book Co., Guwahati, 1964.
12. Kshemendra, *Sagarika* (The Sea), Published by the Author, Guwahati, 1964.
13. Ministry of I and B., *Ladakh*, Government of India, New Delhi, 1965.
14. Ministry of I and B., *Uttar Pub Simanta Agency* (North East Frontier Agency), Government of India, New Delhi, 1966.
15. Baveja, J. Tr. Gogoi, F.C., *Parbate Parbate Bogaba Paro Moi* (Nepal), National Publication Board, Nagaon, 1966.
16. Ministry of I and B., *Jalasinchan aru Vidyut Utpadan* (Irrigation and Power Generation), Government of India, New Delhi, 1966.

17. Dev Sarma, B.K., *Sagar Dekhar Sagar* (Sea Through the Eyes of the Explorers), Bani Prakasani, Calcutta, 1967.
18. Majumdar, L. Tr. Phukan, A., *Amar Nad adi* (Stories about Our Rivers – Part I), National Book Trust, New Delhi, 1970.
19. Chattopadhyay, D. Tr. Goswami, S., *Rahsyamoy Bhayankar* (The Mysterious Danger), P. Goswami, Guwahati, 1971.
20. Das, Manmohan, *Goalpara Jila: Anchalik Boishamayar Bhougolik Vichar* (Goalpara District: A Geographical Study of Regional Disparity), Published by Mrs. A. Das, Guwahati, 1972.
21. Hazarika, A.K., *Dhwansamukhi Prithivi* (The Dying Earth), Monorama Prakash, Jorhat, 1972.
22. Baruah, K.P., *Bhu-bharastar Manuh* (Peoples of the World), Kamala Prakashalay, Guwahati, 1973.
23. Valivappa, L. Tr. Phukan, Yamini, *Amar Nad Nadi* (Our Rivers – Part II), National Book Trust, New Delhi, 1975.
24. Baruah, Kshirdhar, *Sagarar Katha* (Stories about the Oceans), Published by the Author, Biswanath Chariali, Guwahati, 1975.
25. Goswami, R.C., *Sagarar Katha* (About the Oceans), Axom Xahitya Xabha, Jorhat, 1975.
26. Sarma, S., *Nilim Salil Rashi* (The Blue Oceans), Assam Science Society, Guwahati, 1976.
27. Baruah, D., *Chahar Katha* (Stories about Tea), Axom Xahitya Xabha, Jorhat, 1977.
28. Dutta, S.K., *Asomar Khanij Sampad* (Mineral Resources of Assam), Axom Xahitya Xabha, Jorhat, 1978.
29. Gupta, D.K., Tr. Goswami, R.C., *Prithivir Katha* (Story about the Earth), National Book Trust, New Delhi, 1979.
30. Goswami, D.C., *Batar* (The Weather), L.B.S. Publication, Guwahati, 1979.
31. Sarma, J.N., *Asomar Nad Nadi* (The Rivers of Assam), Axom Xahitya Xabha, Jorhat, 1993.

Chapter II

ASSAMESE HISTORICAL WRITING IN THE POST-INDEPENDENCE PERIOD: THEIR EXTENT AND SCOPE

D. Nath

The tradition of writing history in Assamese has been a legacy left by the Ahoms which is being continued even today after the Ahom rule is long over. Maniram Dewan, (Haliram Dhekial Phukan in Bengali), Gunaviram Barua, Padmanath Gohain Barooah and others used to write history in the period after the Ahoms, although by their time history writing in Europe has begun to influence history writing In India as a whole;[1] and this fact has made modern Assamese historical writing distinct from those of the Ahom period, i.e., the *Buranjis* (chronicles).[2] History writing in Assam in the pre and post Independence period of the present century was largely guided by a sense of nationalism, although a trend towards material interpretation of facts has also set in since at least the forties of this century. The scope of writing too has been widened to include various aspects of man's life including those of the lower echelons. In the present paper an attempt has been made to indicate the extent and scope of the major historical works produced in Assamese language in the post-independence period.

The early years of independence were a period of Assamese nationalism. During this period S.K. Bhuyan,

Benudhar Sharma, R.M. Nath and others published a few historical works on subjects concerning Assam. In 1947, S.K. Bhuyan wrote his work *Lachit Barphukan*, which, besides being the biography of the great hero, is a detailed history of the 17th century political condition of Assam. While writing the preface to the work Bhuyan mentions that the objective of writing this history was to infuse national spirit in the minds of his countrymen,[3] which they would derive through the study of the great 17th century Assamese hero. In his other works, e.g., *Buranjir Bani* (1951) *Ramani Gabharu* (1951), *Mir Jumlar Asam Akraman* (1955) and *Konwar Bidroh* (1958) S.K. Bhuyan deals with some important political events of 17th century Assam through which he has tried to find out sources of patriotism with which he desired to imbibe his countrymen. S.K. Bhuyan's important work *Swargadeo Rajeswar Singha* (1975) although a biographical work, is in fact, a serious study of the socio-cultural and political history of 18th century Assam. In his work Bhuyan has not only dealt with the political history of Assam under the rulers of the Tungkhungiya dynasty, but at the same time, he has also enumerated the various arts and crafts pursued by the people of Assam, their relations with the neighbouring hill tribes, and their other cultural pursuits including literature and religion.

Most writings of Benudhar Sharma belonged to this period. A thorough nationalist Benudhar Sharma published his *Satawan Chal Ba Swadhinatar Pratham Yuddha* in 1947, and *Maniram Dewan* in 1950. His *Satawan Chal* is a work on 1857 revolt in India with reference to Assam and as the title indicates Sharma has called and tried to justify it as India's first war of independence. His Maniram Dewan is also a work on the great revolt although apparently it looks like the biography of Maniram Dewan, the 19th century historic figure of Assam. It is here that Benudhar Sharma has emphasised more than due on the role of Maniram Dewan to make him the first martyr of Assam.[4] His other works include *Kangressor Kanchiyali Rodat* (1959), *Arghawali* (1964) and *Dakhinpat Satra* (1967). Benudhar Sharma's autobiography *Majiyar para Mejaloi* (1986) is a storehouse of historical facts for the study of 20th century Assam and the north-east. Besides, in numerous historical articles and speeches published in various Assamese journals,[5] Benudhar Sharma has not only explored various aspects of the political history of Assam from the medieval to the present days, but also very sympathetically brought to light the life and conditions of the common people of this region. Well-versed in every kind of sources for historical studies including folk-lore, Benudhar Sharma however, suffers from lack of historical methodology and undue appreciation of heroes or public figures, such as Maniram Dewan.[6] He also fails to distinguish between history and tradition as he has done in his *Dakhinpat Satra.*[7]

During the early years following independence a few other historians also contributed in their own ways towards the historical writings in Assamese. Among them R.M. Nath's *Bir Chilarai* (1948) and *Gauravmoy Asam* (1949) and his numerous articles and speeches, particularly his presidential speech given at the history section of the Tinsukia session of the Asam Sahitya Sabha, published in various journals and periodicals like the *Asam Sahitya Sabha Patrika, Avahan, Mauchumi, Monideep,* and others, deserve to be mentioned.

Nath's *Bir Chilarai* is till today the only work in Assamese exclusively dealing with the life and works of the great scholar-cum-general of 16th century Assam. In his *Gauraymoy Asam* R.M. Nath has exposed the glorious heritage of early Assam. Not being a historian by profession R.M. Nath is sure to lack in his knowledge of historical methodology but his way of interpreting archaeological sources to write history is an innovation in writing history in Assamese. One of the chief characteristics of his writings Is that he wrote profusely on the life and culture of some of the well known north-eastern tribes and thereby he has reflected on the tribal back-ground of Assamese cultures.[8]

Extreme sense of nationalism has given rise, in the post-Independence period to a distinct class of Assamese historical works; these are histories of certain places or communities. Naturally, they are eulogic. Some of the works of this category of any historic value are Dimbeswar Sarma's *Mangaldoir Buranji* (1961), Benudhar Sharma's *Dakhimat Satra,* mentioned earlier, Tirthanath Sarma's *Auniati Satrar Buranji* (1975), Ramesh Kalita's *Suwalkuchir-Buranji* (1979), Bhabananda Buragohain's *Sadiyar Buranji* (1979) and Nityananda Gogoi's *Buranjiye Parasa*

Biswanath Prantar (1990). Of these works, the *Auniati Satrar Buranji* is a complete history of the Auniati Satra in Majuli, the great royal Vaishnava monastery of Assam. Indeed, this work may be considered as the social and cultural history of the people of the great island-Majuli.[9] Similarly, Nityananda Gogoi's work *Buranjiye-Parasa Biswanath Prantar* is a work on the history of the Biswanath area of Assam based on both archaeological and literary sources. While dealing with other aspects of the history of Biswanath area, Gogoi has thrown Interesting light on the Chulung tribe of Arunachal Pradesh.[10] A similar work entitled *Guwahati Buranjir Khalabamat* (1991) by late Sadananda Chaliha, is a "collection of (the author's) select articles on the antiquity and history of Guwahati and the surrounding tracts", and thus an unconnected short history of the ancient town of Guwahati. It is sure that such micro-level studies have created schisms in the process of social cohesion in the state; but they have helped to restore many of the forgotten aspects of Assam's past history.

Among the works dealing with particular tribe or community mention may be made of Nakul Chandra Bhuyan's *Bara Bhuyanr Buranji* (1960), Sarbananda Rajkumar's, *Chutiya, Bhuyan Aru Matak Rajya* (1965) and *Itihase Sonwara Chasata Bachar* (1980). While Nakul Chandra Bhuyan's work is a history of the Bhuyans of medieval Assam based on tradition and facts, Rajkumar's *Itihase Sonwara Chasata Bachar* is a voluminous history of the Ahoms in Assam, their polity, society and culture. But being guided by emotional urgency, the author's interpretations of facts, such as the reasons for the Ahoms remaining a backward community in Assam at present seems to rest more on his own contention than on genuine historical facts.[11] A few other works, such as the *Mising Sanskritir Alekhya* (enlarged edn. 1989) edited by Bhrigumuni Kagyung, and Bhaben Narzi's *Bodo-Kachari Samaj Aru Sanskriti* (1966) deserve to be mentioned here, while the *Mising Sanskritir Alekhya* is an anthology of articles covering various aspects of the Mising culture written by the well known writers of the tribe, the latter one according to P. Bhattacharya, who introduces the work, is "a critical study of the various aspects of the Bodo-Kachari society and culture in an Indo-Mongoloid back-ground based on actual field material gathered by the writer".[12] There is no doubt that Narzirs' work is a genuine study of the socio-cultural life of the Bodo-Kachari tribe of Assam, but his understanding of the early history of the tribe certainly need to be more refined and objective. In this regard the work *Tribedika* (1986) of Taranath Das and the *Chutiya Jatir Itihas aru Loka Sanskriti* (1991) of Surya Kanta Khanikar - are two significant works, the former one about the *Dalits* (untouchables) and the la or about the Chutiya tribe of Assam. Written from the author's own stand-points both the works rest wore on emotional urgency than historical analysis.

Like other parts of the country, among the Assamese historians too, history is now no longer confined to the study of kings and queens, great men, or to the narration of wars; here too life and conditions of common people, their role in shaping the history of mankind, social, economic and cultural backgrounds of important political events have formed the subject of historical study. Attempt at writing such history is found in H.K. Barpujari's two well known works—*American Missionary Sakal aru Unabingsa Satikar Asam* (1983) and *Asamar Nava-Jagaran: Anaasamiyar Bhumika* (1987). In the first work Barpujari has narrated the role of the American Baptist missionaries in shaping the socio-cultural life of 19th century Assam, and in his second work he depicts the role of the non-Assamese in the 19th century Assamese renaissance. It is clear that Barpujari's selection of subject is very significant and thus, an innovation to the field of historical studies in Assamese, but in certain cases Barpujari's treatment of the subject requires further explanation. For example, in his work *Asamar Nava-Jagaran ... etc.* where he defines a non-Assamese (*Ana-Asamiya*) as one who came to Assam during the 19th century for the purpose of trade and who has settled down here permanently,[13] Barpujari has included among others, the Sikhs, the Muslims and the Manipuris in the list of non-Assamese and thereby he is alleged to have wrongly put-historical facts. At the same time, the astounding historian is very much selective, and he studies the role of only a few very big personalitics (*barmuriya*) only[14] in contradiction of the titles of his works.

Historical writing in Assamese of the post-independence period cover various aspects of men's life. For example,

Banikanta Kakati's work *Prachin Kamrupar Dharmar Dhara* (1955), Maheswar Neog's *Purani Asamiya Samaj aru Sanskriti* (1957), Lila Gogoi's *Tai Sanskritir Ruprekha* (1989) are very specific; society and culture of ancient and medieval Assam being their subjects of study. In his *Prachin Kamrupar Dharmar Dhara* Banikanta Kakati describes the religious practices of the people of Assam in ancient and medieval period till the time of Neo-Vaishnavism of Sankardeva. In his work Kakati, while giving details about religious behaviour of ancient people of the land, has, however, done less exercises to examine the origin and influences of other religious cults than Neo-Vaishnavism of Sankardeva about which he seems to be more sympathetic. Similarly, Maheswar Neog's work too, a social history of the people of early and medieval Assam, betrays disproportionate labour of this great author in dealing with various aspects of religion and society. In main, the work is less concerned to include the culture of the common people as such. Still as pieces of history they are invaluable additions to the Assamese historical studies and may be readily used for any kind of reference in studying Assam's religious and social life of early and medieval period. Lila Gogoi's *Tai Sanskritir Ruprekha* (1961) deals in detail with the life and culture of the Tais, mainly the Ahoms of Assam. The work may justly claim to be an authoritative work on Tai culture in Assam although as a non-professional writer of history Gogoi sometimes fails in application of historical methodology.

In recent years many other works on Assam's socio-cultural life have come out. One of such works is Bap Chandra Mahanta's *Asamiya Jati, Bhasha aru Sahityar Janma Katha* (1996) wherein the astute author has discussed geographical and ethnic factors in analysing the growth of the Assamese community and the Assamese language. In another work, a cultural history of Assam, entitled *Asamar Sanskritik Itihas* (1989) Jatindra Kumar Borgohain has tried to analyse the physical factors behind formation and growth of Assamese culture since early times. One of the important works of recent years is Narayan Chandra Goswami's *Satriya Sanskritir Swarna Rekha* (1994), the golden line of *Satra* culture of Assam, wherein the author of this voluminous work has tried to contribute an improved version of the earlier studies on the Satras, with of course, special reference to the Kamalabari Satra of Majuli which he himself now heads. Published in 1978, Birendra Kumar Bhattacharya's work *Dersa Bacharar Asamiya Sanskriti* is a study of Assam's cultural growth during the British and post-independence period. Aspects dealt with by Bhattacharya in his work include middle class, religion, literature, journalism, fine arts including music and others. Other works dealing with aspects of cultural life in Assam are *Asamar Loka Sanskriti* (1961) of B.K. Barua, *Asamar Loka Kala* (1968) of Jugal Das, *Asamar Nritya Natya Kala* of S.C. Goswami (1978), *Kalbhramar* (1977) and *Asamiya Jatiya Jibanat Mahapurushiya Parampara* (2 Vols. 1987, 1991) of Hiren Gohain, *Unabingsa Satikar Asamat Ebhumuki* (1984) of Prasenjit Choudhury, *Loka Kalpa Dristi* (1987) of Nilamani Phukan, and *Devi* (1986) of Nirmal Prava Bordoloi. Of these works Hiren Gohain's *Mahapurushiya Parampara* and Prasenjit Choudhury's *Unabingsa Satikat Ebhumuki* as pieces of history are very serious works and, thus, are additions to the existing knowledge in this regard. Post-independence Assamese historical writing also includes history of newspapers and journals. In this regard the work *Asamar Batari Kakat: Eti Ruprekha* (1993) of Prafulla Barua, and *Asamar Batari Kakat-Alochanir Dersabachariya Itihas* (1998) which is an anthology of articles contributed by well known writers in the field, deserve to be mentioned here. Both the works deal with the growth of Newspapers and journals in Assam since the days of *Orunodoi*.

Editorials or introductions to some of the best-known Assasmese works form another segment of Assamese historical writings. Thus three important introductions are left by Maheswar Neog in his three well known works: the *Prachya Sasanawali* (compiled and edited, 1974), the *Pavitra Asam* (edited, 1960) which is a "descriptive account of the holy places of Assam", and the *Gurucharit Katha* (edited, 1986), the most voluminous biographical work of the medieval Vaishnava saints of Assam. Similarly, his introduction to the *Orunodoi*, the first Assamese newspaper (1846), is an invaluable addition to the study of 19th century Assam. Few other editorials of any historical value are to be found in the *Asam Bandhu* (re-edited & compiled by Nagen Saikia, 1984), the *Katha-Guru Charit* (edited by Upen Chandra Lekharu, 1952), and the

Darrang Raj Vamsavali (edited by Nabin Chandra Sharma, (1973),

As against the traditional conception applied to the study of Assam's socio-cultural history, its study in post-independence period has been taken up also by some writers who are largely influenced by the materialist conception of history. Bishnu Prasad Rabha, Bhabananda Dutta, Amlendu Guha, Hiren Gohain, Dhrubajyoti Bora may be included among this group of writers. Beginning to write since the early forty's Bishnu Prasad Rabha in his *Asamiya Kristir Chamu Abhash* (1946) has pointed out that Assamese culture would thrive only when the cultures of the ethnic groups inhabiting the land are preserved and encouraged. Following Rabha, Bhabananada Dutta wrote a series of articles in *Jayanti*, an Assamese monthly, on the history and culture of Assam towards the last part of the 40's. In fact, Bhabananda Dutta can be said to have formally introduced the methodology of economic interpretations in history to explain production relations and social changes. In the seventies of the present century Amalendu Guha wrote a few articles, such as the 'Samanta Yugiya Asamar Bhumi Vyavastha aru Samajr Sreni' (*Natun Prithivi*, 1972), 'Vaishnavbadar Para Mayamara Bidrohaloi' (a series of articles published in *Amar Pratinidhi*, 1976–79) etc. wherein Guha has analysed the production processes and production relations in Assam under the Ahoms to explain the root of the Mayamara revolt and to show that it was a class-struggle.[15] Guha's articles have now been compiled and published under the title *Vaishnavbadar Para Mayamara Bidrohaloi* (1993). Another work of Amalendu Guha is *Jamidarkalin Goalpara Jilar Artha Samajik Abastha: Eti Aitihasik Dristipat* (1984). In this work Guha has discussed the conditions of certain zamindars in Goalpara district after the Permanent Settlement in 1793. Here the author has given a picture of the relations between the zamindars and their Garo peasants.

Following Amalendu Guha, Dhrubajyoti Bora wrote his *Moamariya Gana Abhyutthan* (1983) where he has attempted to show that the revolt was a peasant movement.[16] Although a serious study on the great 18th century revolt of Assam, Bora's work suffers from certain methodological draw backs. Other historical works produced by writers of this class include those of Hiren Gohain (such as *Kal Bhramar* mentioned earlier), Prasenjit Choudhury (*Unabingsa Satikar Asamat Ebhumuki, Asamar Chah Banua Aru Unais Satikar Vidvat Samaj*, 1989), Prafulla Mahanta (*Asamar Madhya-bitta Srenir Itihas*, 1991), Lakshminath Tamuli (*Bharatar Swadhinata Sangramat Asamar Avadan*, 1988), Jatindra Kumar Borhgohain (*Asamar Arthanaitik Itihas*, 1985), etc. Of these works Prasenjit Choudhury's *Asamar Chah Banua ... etc.* is indeed a pioneering work in Assamese on the tea garden labourers of Assam. Prior to this work only Nakul Chandra Bhuyan wrote in 1960 his *Chah Baganar Banua*. Lakshmi Nath Tamuly's work *Bharatar Swadhinata Sangramat Asamar Abadan* is a detailed history of Assam's role in the freedom struggle of India, although much emphasis has been given on the role of the plains people and the middle classes only.[17] Similarly, Prafulla Mahanta's work *Asamiya Madhya-bitta Srenir Itihas*, a Ph.D. thesis of Gauhati University, is a detailed history of the 19th and 20th century Assamese middle class, their role in the growth of Assamese literature and culture, their class character and their socio-political organisations.

In recent years women's studies have been undertaken as an important aspect of historical writing in Assamese. The journal *Aideur Jonaki Bat* edited by Aparna Dutta Mahanta, is a pioneering work in this regard where valuable articles from Assamese writers, such as Swarnalata Barua, Aparna Dutta Mahanta, and many others are serially published. One of the important works in the field is Dipti Sarma's *Mukti Yujat Luitpariya Nari* (1995) where the author has discussed the role of women of the Brahmaputra Valley in the freedom struggle of India. This work is a summary translation of her Ph.D. thesis on the same subject submitted to the Gauhati University. An important aspect of the work is that the author here has duly emphasised on the role of Assamese women of all classes and all sections including women of tea garden communities.

Much light has been thrown on history of Assam through the publication of a series of biographical literature in Assamese. Maheswar Neog's *Sri Sri Sankardev* (1948), Benudhar Sharma's *Maniram Dewan* (1951) deserve to be mentioned in this regard. Neog's *Sri Sri Sankardev* is a well-researched work dealing with the life and works of the great Vaishnava reformer of Assam of the middle ages and at the same time, throwing much light on the contemporary history of the state. Benudhar Sharma's *Maniram Dewan*, in spite of being a biographical work, is a history of 19th century Assam. His other biographical work *Gangagovinda Phukan* (1948) along with Prafulla Dutta Goswami's *Manik Chandra Barua Aru Teor Yug* throw much light on the history of the middle class in modern Assam. Similar works of historical value include *Piyali Phukan Aru Sei Samay* by Bhuban Chandra Sandikoi (1957), *Yuganayak Sankardev* by Dimbeswar Neog (1977), *Sainik Silpi Bishnu Rabha* by Hiren Gohain (1982), *Sipahi Bidroh Aru Parbatiya Barua* by Golokeswar Barua (1974) and *Sankardev: Kriti Aru Krititta* by Sibanath Barman (1986). These and other biographical works including the autobiography of Benudhar Sharma—*Majiyar para Mejaloi* (1986), although not historical works in proper sense, are valuable additions to the study of 20th century history of Assam in Assamese.

From the above it can be said that the tradition of writing history in Assam and in Assamese has been carried on without much interruption even after the Ahoms who laid this tradition in the land about 13th century A.D. Significantly, Assamese historians have readily reacted to the modern developments in historiography. At the same time the scope of historical studies have also been considerably widened beyond the life of the kings, queens, great men and the description of their warfare. Historical writings now include almost all aspects of human life, such as political, cultural, social and economic; important works are being done on the various social classes, the freedom struggle, student movement or women affairs. As a result, Assamese historical writings have naturally given rise to various schools of thought, such as nationalist or materialist. The only unhealthy aspect that one can notice in the volumes of historical production is that often historians are guided by what is termed as back-door nationalism,[18] or more properly communalism. At the same time, scope of the post-independence Assamese historical writings are largely limited to the study of Assam of the modern period alone, and that too mostly concerned with the caste society only.

Tribal studies are almost neglected; and barring a few works, most others are not concerned about the tribal background of Assamese culture. It is to be noted that contributions of the ethnic, tribes, backward communities or Scheduled Caste have been falling apart from historians notice. Very little has been done at the same time, on hills and plains relations, on the Barak Valley or on the early history of the region of north-east India.

Notes and References

1. R.C. Majumdar, *Historiography in Modern India*, Calcutta etc., 1970, pp. 1ff; Prafulla Dutta Goswami, *Manik Chandra Barua*, Guwahati, 1977, p. 5.
2. H.K. Barpujari, *Itihas: Rachanabidhi aru Kramabikash*, Guwahati, 1988, for details; D. Nath, 'Buranji Sahitya' in H. Borgohain (ed.) *Asamiya Sahityar Buranji*, Vol. VI, Guwahati, 1993, p. 506.
3. 2nd Print, Guwahati, 1980, pp. 10f.
4. H. Gohain, Introduction to *Benudhar Sharma Rachanawali*, Vol. II, Guwahati, 1987, p. III; T.N. Sharma, *Benudhar Sarma*, Guwahati, 1983, p. 146; *Asamiya Sahityar Buranji*, Vol. VI, p. 220.
5. For his various articles and speeches see *Benudhar Sharma Rachanawali* (Vols. III & IV), Guwahati, 1987.
6. H. Gohain, Introduction, *loc.cit.*, pp. XVI-XX.
7. See pp. 40ff.
8. For details see his English work *Background of Assamese Culture*, Shillong, 1948, and various articles published in journals and periodicals. Also see, Barpujari, *Itihas: Rachanabidhi*, p. 166.
9. For the history of the Majuli Island reference may be made to D. Nath's several articles published in various Assamese periodicals including the one entitled 'Luitar Majuli—Majuli Dvip: Iyar Sristi aru Aitihasik Avasthan' (the Majuli island—its geographical history and antiquity), published in the *Souvenir*, on the occasion of the XIV session of the NEIHA at Jorhat, 1993, pp. 81–87.
10. Pp. 106ff.
11. See, p. 907.
12. Cf. Introduction, p. 11.
13. See p. 4.
14. Ibid.
15. Cf. Introduction to the *Vaishnavbadar Para Mayamara Bidrohaloi.*
16. *Ibid*; also Bora's work, pp. 115, 169.
17. See *Asamiya Sahityar Buranji*, Vol. VI, pp. 519f.
18. Referred to by Bipan Chandra in *Communalism and the Writing of Indian History* (4th print), New Delhi, 1984, p. 48.

A Short Bibliography of Hisatories in Assamese

Barbaruah, Hiteswar : *Ahomar Din*, Guwahati, 1981.

Borgohain, Homen (ed.) : *Asamiya Sahityar Buranji* (Vol. VI), Guwahati, 1993.

Borgohain, Jatindra Kr. : *Asamar Sanskriti*, Golaghat, 1989.

: *Asamar Arthanaitik Itihas*, Jorhat, 1985.

Barua, B.K. : *Asamar Loka Sanskriti*, Guwahati, 1961.

: *Asamiya Bhasha aru Sanskriti*, Guwahati, 1957.

Barua, Prafulla : *Asamar Batari Kakat: Eti Ruprekha*, Guwahati, 1993.

Barpujari, H.K. : *American Missionary Sakal aru Unabingsa Satikar Asam*, Jorhat, 1983.

: *Asamar Navajagaran: Ana-Asamiyar Bhumika*, Jorhat, 1987.

Barman, Sibnath : *Sankardev: Kriti Aru Krititta*, Guwahati, 1986.

: *Srimanta Sankardev Aru Teor Yugar Vaishnavacharya Sakal*, Guwahati, 1993.

(ed) : *Asamiya Sahityar Buranji* (Vol. II), Guwahati, 1997.

Bhuyan, S.K. : *Asam Buranj. Katha*, Guwahati, 1989 (Collection of articles written between 1931–1947)

: *Lachit Barphukan*, Guwahati, 1971, 1980.

: *Swargadeo Rajeswar Simha*, Guwahati, 1975.

: *Mir Jumlar Asam Akraman*, Guwahati, 1955.

: *Ramani Gabharu*, Guwahati, 1951.

: *Konwar Bidroh*, Guwahati, 1958.

: *Buranjir Bani*, Guwahati, 1951.

Bhuyan, Jogendra Narayan : *Sadagar Bholanath Barooah*, Diphu, 1993.

Bhuyan, Jogendra Narayan : *Unabingsa Satikar Asam Sangbad*, Dibrugarh University, 1990.

Bhuyan, Gunindra Nath (ed) : *Charaideo*, Guwahati, 1988.

Bora, Dhrubajyoti : *Moamariya Gana Abhutthwan*, Guwahati, 1983.

Buragohain, Bhabananda : *Sadiyar Buranji*, Guwahati, 1983.

Buragohain, Hem : *Jaimati Kunwari*, Sibsagar, 1993.

Bhattacharya, Birendra Kr. : *Dersabacharar Asamiya Sanskritit Ebhumuki*, Guwahati, 1978.

Chaliha, Sadananda : *Guwahati Buranjir Khalabamat*, Guwahati, 1991.

Choudhury, Prasenjit : *Samaj Aru Sanskriti*, Nalbari, 1983.

: *Atit Amesandhan*, Nalbari, 1990.

: *Asamar Chah Barua aru Unaib Satikar Bidvat Samaj*, Dibrugarh, 1989.

Das, Taranath : *Tribedika*, Sibsagar, 1986.

Dutta, Bhabananda : *Asamiyar Jatiya Samasyar Bibartan*, Guwahati, 1986.

Dutta, Birendranath : *Asamiya Sangitar Aitijya*, Jorhat, 1977.

Dutta, D.K. et.al. (ed.) : *Chinta aru Chinta*, Jorhat, 1995 (Collection of Historical and Literary articles).

Gogoi, Lila : *Belimar Gol*, Dibrugarh, 1983.

: *Tai Sanskritir Ruprekha*, Guwahati, 1961.

Gogoi, Nomal : *Mayamara Samaj-Sanskritir Ruprekha*, Tinsukia, 1990.

Gogoi, Pushpa : *Tai Sanskriti*, Dhemaji, 1994.

Gogoi, Thanuram : *Tai-Jatir Prachin Dharma aru Samaj Niti*, Guwahati, 1984.

Gogoi, Nityananda : *Buranjie Parasha Bishwanath Prantar*, Bishwanath Chariali, 1990.

Gohain, Hiren : *Asamiya Jatiya JibanatMahapurushiya Parampara* (2 Vols.) Vol. I, Guwahati, 1987; II, Guwahati, 1991.

Goswami, Prafulla Duta : *Asamiya Jana Sahitya*, Guwahati, 1948.

: *Baramahar Terageet*, Guwahati, 1962.

: *Manik Chandra Barua Aru Teonr Yug*, Guwahati, 1970.

Goswami, Narayanchandra : *Satriya Sanskritir Swarnarekha*, Natun Kamalabari Satra, 1994.

Guha, Amalendu : *Vaishnavbadar Para Mayamariya Bidrohaloi*, Guwahati, 1993.

: *Jamidarkalin Goalpara Jilar Artha-Samajik Avastha*, Dhubri, 1984.

Handique, Bhuban Chandra : *Piyali Phukan Aru Sei Samaito*, Jaisagar, 1957.

Kagyung, Bhrigumuni : *Mishing Sanskritir Alekhya*, Guwahati, 1989.

Kakati, Banikanta : *Banikanta Rachanawali* (ed.) M. Neog, (Assamese Volume), Guwahati, 1991.

: *Prachin Kamrupar Dharmar Dhara*, Pathsala, 1953.

Kalita, Benudhar : *Phulagurir Dhewa*, Nagaon, 1961.

Kalita, Ramesh : *Bharatar Swadhinata Sangramat Asamiya Chatrar Bhumika*, Nalbari, 1986.

Kalita, Ramesh Chandra : *Sualkuchir Buranji*, Sualkuchi, 1979.

Khanikar, Surya Kanta : *Chutiya Jatir Itihas Aru Loka Sanskriti* (2 Vols.), Guwahati, 1991.

Lekharu, Upendra Ch. (ed) : *Katha Guru Charit*, Nalbari, 1952.

Mahanta, Bap Chandra : *Asamiya Jati, Bhasha Aru Sahityar Janmakatha*, Jorhat, 1996.

Mahanta, Prafulla : *Asamiya Madhyabitta Shreneer Itihas*, Guwahati, 1991.

Narzi, Bhaben : *Bodo-Kacharir Samaj Aru Sanskriti*, Kokrajhar, 1966.

Nath, Rajmohan : *Bir Chilarai*, Shillong, 1948.

: *Gauravmay Asam*, Shillong, 1949.

Nath, Dambarudhar : *Asam Buranji*, Guwahati, 1988.

Natun Sahitya Parishad : *Asamar Sramik Andolan*, Itihas Aru Dhara, Guwahati, 1993.

Neog, Dimbeswar : *Yuganayak Sankardev*, Guwahati, 528 Sankarabda.

Neog, Maheswar (ed.) : *Prachya Sasanawali*, Guwahati, 1974.

(ed.) : *Guru Charit Katha*, Gauhati University, 1986.

(ed.) : *Orunodoi*, Guwahati, 1983.

(ed.) : *Pavitra Asam*, Jorhat, 1969.

: *Purani Asamiya Samaj Aru Sanskriti*, Dibrugarh, 1957.

: *Asamar Dharmar Buranji*, Jorhat, 1990.

: *Orunodoi Sambad Patra*, Guwahati, 1993.

Prastab Gosthi : *Sankardevar Chintat Pragatisilata*, Dibrugarh, 1983.

Rabha, Bishnu Prasad : *Asamiya Krishtir Chamu Abhas*, Guwahati, 1946.

Sarma, Pradip : *Asamar Bilupta Maidam Parampora*, Guwahati, 1993.

Sarma, Tirthanath : *Auniati Satrar Buranji*, Auniati, 1977.

Sastri, Manoranjan : *Purani Asamar Dharma Aru Darshan*, Guwahati, 1986.

Sharma, Benudhar : *Benudhar Sharma Rachanavali* (Vol. II), Guwahati, 1987.

: *Majiyar Para Majaloi*, Guwahati, 1986.

: *Chandan Chara*, Guwahati, 1987.

: *Tokora Bahhar Kuta*, Guwahati, 1987.

Sharma, Giridhar (ed.) : *Asamiya Jatir Itibritta*, Jorhat, 1974.

Sharma, Nabinchandra : *Darang Raj Vamsawali*, Guwahati, 1973.

Tamuli, Lakshminath (ed.) : *Bharatar Swadhinata Sangramat Asamar Avadan*, Guwahati, 1988.

Saikia, Nagen (ed.) : *Asam Bandhu*, Dibrugarh, 1984.

Chapter III

NUMISMATIC STUDIES IN ASSAMESE

S.K. Bose

Use of coins for day to day transactions in Assam started only as late as the mid-17th Century, when Ahoms introduced rupee-coins in their kingdom. Later on, small denomination silver coins were also introduced by them.[1] In a correspondence dated 27.05.1834, between the Fort William Authority at Calcutta and their counterpart in Assam, states the Assamese populace to be habituated in the use of small silver coins. These ranged in denomination a rupee down to silver half anna pieces.[2]

Despite such a backdrop, numismatic studies had not been reflected properly in Assamese language; at least not to our expectation. It is all the more painful that even though among all the major Indian linguistic publications, an Assamese magazine *Orunodoi* was probably the first to introduce numismatics to its readers as early as 1850 A.D., its efforts were not sustained. It is however, true that old manuscripts (buranjis) refer to coins by the Ahom rulers and even the management of mints.[3]

Orunodoi stood apart among the early vernacular journals in India.[4] It was first published in January, 1846, from Sibsagar (Assam) and was edited by Mr N. Brown, an American baptist missionary. Besides its sections on religion, science and intelligence, it was perhaps the only publication of its kind to cater to numismatics from 1850, but with faithful regularity only from July 1854. The material therein referred to hoard—finds, forgeries, and various related topics, supplemented by facsimiles of coins. Although all the copies of the magazine after December 1854 could not be traced, there is reason to believe that publication of numismatic information certainly continued beyond December, 1854.

The magazine had not restricted itself only to Assamese coins. Between 1846 and 1854 A.D. *Orunodoi* illustrated as many as one hundred eight coins, tokens and seals (see below). It had covered six hoards and two cases of forgery of coins. It is unfortunate that the names of the contributors have not been mentioned. It was not a mean achievement with a limited circulation and the given environment.

COINS	-	106
Ahom	-	65
Mughal	-	13
Sultans	-	16
Koch	-	4
Bikaner	-	2
Manipur	-	1
Jaintia	-	1
Foreign	-	4
SEALS	-	1
TOKENS	-	1
Total	-	108

Despite the fact that the Ahom coins are very interesting from the angle of artistic ecstacy, minting technology and calligraphy, they failed to receive due attention either from the scholars or the numismatists of the region. As a result, within the span of a century after *Orunodoi* was discontinued, hardly any serious numismatic articles were published. The few that were published were mere repetitions.[5] Exceptions ofcourse prevail, as when a chapter or a page in a book contained useful numismatic information. Satyendra Nath Sharma's *Swadhinata Surjyar Kramakshiyaman Poharat Axom Buranji* is one such example. Sarbanand Rajkumar's *Itihase Sowara Chashata Bachor* is another. *Ahomor Din* by Hiteswar Barbarua details the role of the mint (*Rup Mara shal*) employees. An important note on coins can also be seen in Jatin Borgohain's *Axomor Arthanaitik Itihas* (Jorhat, 1985).

We now append references of articles published in Assamese journals and papers:

i) 'Buranji Sabhar Sabhapatir Abhibhaxan' by Hiteswar BarBarua, (*Ghar Jeoti*, 2nd Year, 6th Issue, 1850 Saka (1928 A.D.) gives us some important information about the sources of gold and silver in Assam, which had helped the Ahoms to strike their coins.

ii) 'Toka-Paicha', by Jitendra Nath Das, *Abahan*, 11th Year, 10th issue, *Aswin, Saka* 1862 (1940 A.D.), pp. 1028-1031. This was the first of the series of articles written by the same author covering various aspects of money and its utility as medium of exchange. However, this article can not be regarded as numismatic article in a true sense.

iii) 'Ahom Rojar Mudra' by Sarbananda Rajkumar, *Bahi*, 29 years *Bhad*. 1864 Saka (1942 A.D.) has covered elaborately the Ahom coins and can be treated as useful reference. This was followed by his article 'Ahom Rajasokoror Mudra', *Tai Sonskriti*, Vol. I, 1956, on the same line.

iv) 'Axomor Prachin Mudra', by Murari Charan Das, *Jayanti*, 6th issue, 1953, pp.420-422. The author has highlighted the coins issued by the Rulers of Assam, Koch Behar, Jaintia, Manipur and also narrates "Jabeli Coins" (token?) of the Ao Nagas.

v) 'Dhulapadung Cha Bagisat Aviskrita Mudra' by S. Bhattacharya, *Dainik Asom* dated 27.11.1977. This article was the first to throw light on the most meaningful discovery of 9th Century Copper Coins of Assam.

vi) 'Uttar-Pub Bharator Mudra Adhyanar Parichaya by R.D. Choudhury, *Asom Sahitya Patrika* (II) 1978, narrates the progress of numismatic studies in N.E. India and also focuses on future prospects for further studies.

vii) 'Prachin Aru Adi—Madhyajugor Axomor Mudra Byabastha' by Tarak Chandra Goswami, *Gariyoshi*, Vol. I, No. 6, March 1994. The author in this article has highlighted the limited use of coins during the related period. According to him pieces of gold, silver, cowrie, elephant, horse, cow, goat, animal skin and cloth etc. served the role of medium of exchange. However, the existence of 9th Century copper coins and Kachari coins prior to Yashonarayana had probably escaped his notice.

viii) S.K. Bose also published two articles dealing with tea garden tokens and their use; (a) 'Engraj Rajattat Axomor Cha Bagisat Darmaha Dia Paddhati', *Ahom Sahitya Sabha Patrika,* 3rd issue, 1994-95, Guwahati; (b) 'Axomor Cha Bagisar Mudra', *Pratik,* 1-15 Oct, 1994, Guwahati. In this paper we have not covered simple references made in numerous books, magazines and papers for obvious reasons. The author, despite his earnest desire, could also not look up all the copies of *Orunodoi, Bahi, Jonaki, and Usha,* wherein articles on coins might have appeared. Interestingly, In *Abahan's* 1st Yr., 5th issue (1851 Saka, 1893 A.D.), there is a reference of Late Rajendra Narayan Choudhury, Mechpara, Lakshipur, Goalpara, as a numismatist.

Reference

1. Rhodes N., *The Coinage of North East India,* Hythe, 1994, p.131-174.
2. Author's 'Demonetisation in 19th Century Assam', *Proceedings of NEIHA,* 1997.
3. Many of the old manuscripts written in Ahom and Assamese were subsequently translated or edited, and printed. Prominent among these are *Tungakhungia Buranji* (Tr. by S.K. Bhuyan), *Purani Assam Buranji* (Edited by Hem Chandra Goswami), *Assam Buranji* (Kasi Nath Tamuli Phukan), *Assam Buranji* (by Hara Kanta Barua Sadar Amin), *Deodhai Asam Buranji* (Edited by S.K. Bhuyan), *Kachari Buranji, Jainta Buranji* and *Kamrupar Buranji* (all edited by S.K. Bhuyan) and *Darrang Raj Vansavali* (Edited by N.C.Sarma).
4. *Orunodoi* 1846-1854, Edited by C.P. Saikia, 1983 (reprint), Guwahati.
5. Talks on Numismatics, *The Sentinel* (daily), Guwahati, 25.10.94.

Chapter IV

FOLKLORE STUDIES ON NORTH-EAST INDIA IN BENGALI LANGUAGE (1947–97)

Amalendu Bhattacharjee

The North East region of India is the abode of different ethnic groups which has made the region an ideal ground for anthropological and folkloristic research. In this region research in folklore in Bengali Language was initiated in 1915. Noted historian Padmanath Bhattacharjee published a collection of proverbs of Surma-Barak Valley in *Sreebhumi* (Ist year, 11th issue, Falgun 1322 B.E.), a monthly literary journal published from Karimganj. Since then a very large number of papers and a few books on folklore have been published. In the pre-independence period three journals took upon themselves the task of publishing articles and papers on the subject. These journals were: (a) the *Sreehatta Sahitya Parisat Patrika* (1936) published from Sylhet, (b) the *Quarterly Sikshasevak* (1925) and (c) the monthly *Vijyini* (1940), both published from Silchar.

In the period following the independence the branches of the study of folklore have been further enriched. Folkloristics has become a recognised branch of academic pursuit and for research work in this sphere well marked and accepted methodology is being used. This has resulted in a qualitative change in the studies of folklore.

During the half century since independence, as many as seventeen books on folklore of the North East have been published of which the following six are the anthologies of folksongs.

1. Dutta Gurusaday & Bhowmick, Nirmalendu (ed.), *Sree-hatter Lok Sangeet*, Calcutta University, 1966.
2. Bhattacharjee, Amalendu (ed.), *Barak Upatyakar Baramasi Gan*, Cachar Banga Sahitya O Sanskriti Sammelan, Silchar, 1984.
3. Bhattacharjee, Jatindra Mohan & Choudhury, Bijan Krishna (ed.), *Baul Kavi Radharaman geeti Sangraha*, Saraswati Book Depot, Agartala, 1988.
4. Bhattacharjee, Jatindra Mohan (Ed), *Sreehatter bhatta Sangeet*, Bangiya Jatiya Siksha Parishad, Jatindra Mohan Sangrahasala, Calcutta -32, 1989.
5. Chakraborty, Ajoy Kumar (ed.), *Sonarayer Gan*, Goalpara, Assam.
6. Chanda, Prasanna Kumar, *Kavi Geetikanjali*, Soroshi Printers, Park Road, Silchar, undated.

The materials for *Sreehatter Lok Sangeet* have been collected by Gurusaday Dutta. He collected the material from thirty-six folk singers and submitted the work to Cacutta University on September 3rd, 1939. It is worth mentioning that most of these singers belonged to the present district of Karimganj. This work was published in book form by Nirmalendu Bhowmick in 1966. This book has three parts - Introduction, Collection and Appendix. Although in the original work there were 423 songs, 43 of these have been dropped in the published book. The title of the book is somewhat misleading because all sorts of folksongs have not been represented in it. Sreehatta or Sylhet has been incorporated into erstwhile East Pakistan, now Bangladesh, but a part of the Karimganj Subdivision of the Sylhet district now is a district in Southern Assam. The Barak Valley and Sylhet bear the same folk tradition, a fact which makes this book so important in the study of the folklore of Barak Valley. In the appendix of the book have been reprinted articles which had been published in magazines and journals that are rare now. The notation of a song and the text of another song transcribed in International Phonetic alphabet have also been printed in this book.

Barak Upatyakar Baramasi Gan is an anthology of twenty Baramasi Songs. At the end of each song the name and address of the source from where it has been collected and the meaning of dialect words have been given. In the Introduction of the book the origin of *Baramasi* songs has been discussed.

Baul Kavi Radharaman Geeti Sangraha is a collection of songs composed by Radharaman Dutta (1834-1916), who is called the sage poet of Barak-Surma Valley. He bade adieu to family and society and embraced the life of *Sannyas*. A sage of the *Sahajiya* cult, he composed more than a thousand songs and earned great popularity. 898 of the songs in the collection are arranged according to the classification of Vaishnava literature. Biographical details of the poet, comments on the literary merits of and references to local affairs in the songs have been added in the introductory part of the collection. In the appendix we find the lineage and autobiographical verses etc. of Radharaman.

Sreehatter Bhatta Sangeet is a collection of 38 poems composed by 17 Bhatta poets. A group of persons titled Bhattas composed poetry according to certain technique are known as Bhatta Sangeet. At a later date some Muslim poets also composed Bhatta poetry. The subject matter of Bhatta poetry are classified as (a) Mythological, and (b) Narration of contemporary events. The second class of this kind of poetry may be considered more important in as much as it has historical value because of the references to earthquake, flood, economic depression, robbery etc. incorporated in it. The poems in this collection were collected originally by the noted historian Padmanath Bhattacharjee Vidyabinod. In the introductory part short biographies of the Bhatta poets have been given. Padmanath Bhattacharjee's article rich for its information about the Bhatta poets, has been reprinted in the Appendix.

Sona Roy is the popular Tiger-deity in the Goalpara district in Western part of Assam. This deity is worshipped by the cattle-grazers during Magh Bihu wishing the welfare of the cattle wealth. A long narrative poem relating to Sona Roy has been incorporated in the book *Sonaroyer Gan*.

Kavi Geetikanjali is a collection of 36 Kavi Gans among

which *Jalplavan* narrating the deluge of 1929, and others such as *Biyer Gan, Kanyaday, deser dasa* etc. are quite important. But there is much to be desired in the matter of editing.

The other books on folklore are:

1. Chakraborty, Sashimohan (Ed), *Sreehatiya Prabad Prabachan*, Sreehatta Sammilani, 12 Hindustan Road, Calcutta-29, 1970.
2. Biswas, Hemanga, *Lok Sangeet Samiksha Bangla O Assam*, A Mukherjee & Co.Pvt.Ltd., 2—Bankim Chatterjee Street, Calcutta-73, 1978.
3. Chakraborty, Puranjan Prasad, *Rajmala O Adhunik, Tripura*, Hemanta Basu Sarani, Agartala, 1985.
4. Dey, Dr Ranjit, *Tripurar Lok-Jeevan O Loksanskriti*, Nabajatak Prakashan, A/64 College Street Market, Calcutta-7, 1986.
5. Choudhury, Sujit, *Prachin Bharate Matripradhanya, Kimbadantir Punarbichar, Pyapirus*, 2-Ganendra Mitra Lane, Calcutta-14, 1990.
6. Ahmed, Kamaluddin, *Sanskritir Rong-Rup*, Digbalay Prakashan, Karimganj, Assam, 1990.
7. Nath, Prabash Chandra, *Barak Upatyakar Bangla Lok Sahitya*, Academy Research Institute, South Bekirpar, Cachar, Assam, 1993.
8. Bhattacharjee, Mukundadas, *Barak Upatyakar Lok Nritya*, Gramin Nrityakala, Baul-Loknritya Prachar Samity, Central Road, Silchar-1, Assam, 1995.
9. Basu, Sibtapan, *Tista Baraker Laukik Devata*, Akshar Sahitya Prakashan, Bipin Paul Road, Karimganj, Assam, 1995.
10. Amiya Bandapadhyay, *Barak Upatyakar Bangali Hindu Samajer Bibaher Chalchitra*, Lala, Dist. Hailakandi, Assam, 1995.
11. Tapadar, Jahid Ahmed, *Dimacha Lok Katha*, Nikhil Bharat Banga Sahitya Sammelan, Halflong Branch, Halflong, 1996.

Sreehattiya Prabad Prabachan is a collection of 1704 Local proverbs and adages. Different texts of these, wherever found, have also been added over and above the references to similar proverbs and adages in other Languages. The collection may be considered valuable.

Lok Sangeet Samiksha Bangla O Assam is written by the prominent folk singer Hemanga Biswas. Altogether, sixteen subject-matters related to folk songs have been discussed in the book. The first twelve chapters - A few modern problems of folk songs, War and peace as narrated in folk songs, Dialect and pronunciation in folk-songs etc. are mostly theoretical analysis. The other chapters deal with Bihu songs. The author of the book was a dedicated organiser of Indian Peoples Theatre group. As a result, he has emphasised on Marxian interpretation. A subjective write-up on the legendary dhol player Maghai Ojha has also been included in the book.

In the book *Rajmala O Adhunik Tripura* the history of Tripura has been primarily studied, though briefly. Side by side a variety of other subjects like *Ker Puja*, the worship of folk deities, the folk life of the Tripuris and the folk art of Tripura have been discussed in a brief manner in which, however, there is a plethora of information.

A detailed study of the ancient history of Tripura, the identity of various ethnic groups, folk literature and ritual has been made in the book *Tripurar Lokjeevan O Loksanskriti*. Enriched with various data and quotations, this book is representative of the folklore studies of Tripura.

Prachin Bharate Matripradhanya: Kimbadantir Punarbichar is a research work of high standard. A collection of four papers, the subjects discussed in the book are the legend of Savitri-Satyaban, the worship of Kartika, the source and backdrop of the Vrihannala legend and mother Lineage in ancient India. Multi-disciplinary approach is a special quality of the book. The originality of the author lies in the manner in which he has analysed the customs prevalent in Barak valley in a wide perspective.

Sanskritir Rongrup contains three articles of which Barak Upatyakar Musalmander Sanskritik uttaradhikar and *Barak Upatyakar Loksanskritir Islami Uttaradhikare Vaisnab Prabhab* are concerned with folklore. In both the articles the traditional folkculture of the Muslims and the significance of cultural unification have been discussed.

Barak Upatyakar Bangla Lok Sahitya is a collection of nine articles dealing with a variety of subjects like Rhymes, folk-tales, proverbs, Riddles, Marriage songs and Ritual Rhymes.

But one grave loophole of the book is that references to the sources of the used materials have not been given.

In the book *Barak Upatyakar Loknritya: Gramin Nrityakala*, the author, who is himself a folk dancer, has dealt with a few forms of local folk dance. As a performing artist he has mainly discussed the performance of these dance forms. But in the book there is a conspicuous absence of adherence to any methodology.

The book *Tista Baraker Laukik Devata* is divided into two parts in the first of which the folk deities of North Bengal and in the second, those of Barak Valley have been discussed. In the discussion on the folk deities of Barak Valley, the author has incorporated local rites and rituals. In the work references to the sources of the materials have not been given.

Barak Upatyakar Bangali Hindu Samaje Bibaher Chalchitra is a book on the marriage rites of the region. But the discussion of the rites is incomplete in the sense that mainly the marriage rites of the middle class have been discussed. But the classification and varieties of marriage rites springing from differences in Socio-economic status and caste-system have not been dealt with.

Dimacha Lokkatha is a collection of ten animal tales. These are directly translated from Dimacha Language to Bengali. The motifs of the tales have not been referred to. The value of the book lies in the fact that it is the first book of Dimacha tales translated into Bengali.

Besides books a large number of articles on the subject have been written. It is necessary to mention that no regular research journal is published in Bengali language in the North-Eastern region of the country. Naturally the articles have been published in the different periodicals. Some little magazines, however, published special issues on folklore. Two such magazines are:

(a) *Akshar Britta*, 2nd year. 3rd Vol. August, 1992, Ed. Kapish Kanti Dey, Bipin Paul Road, Karimganj, Assam.
(b) *Prabha*, 5th year, Joint issue, December 1991 and January, 1992, Mahaprabhu Sarani, P.O. Lala, Hailakandi Dist. Assam.

The general subject matter of the special issue of *Akshar Britta* is Manasa cult in Barak Valley. The particular subjects dealt with in the five articles in the issue are the Backdrop and Origin of Manasa worship, description of various rites associated with Manasa, the ritual tale of Nagpanchami, the influence of Manasa on folkart. The people who place before the audience the greatness of Manasa through songs and dance performance are popularly called *Ojha*. In the issue an interview with an 'Ojha' has also been published. The well written articles, supported by Sketches, may be of great value to the researchers.

Ten articles have been published in *Prabaha* in which such subjects as *Sankata*— a folk deity of Barak Valley, Songs of *Gaji, Dhamail* dance, social picture in folk songs, Universality of folk tale, Folk poet Hachan Raja, Ritual Rhyme —*Ai*, History and Legend, Cultural life of the Bengalees, Folk literature of Barak Valley have been dealt with.

In the dailies, half-weeklies, weeklies, periodicals and literary magazines a large number of articles on folklore have been published all of which may not be regarded as research papers. It is worth mentioning that folklore is the creation of the traditional life style and mental endeavours of the people. The folklore is generally classified as (a) Material Folklore and (b) Formalised Folklore.

The subjects that come under Material Folklore are the human habitats, implements of agriculture and domestic life, garments etc. Folk literature, folkart, folkdance, customs and beliefs fall under the second class i.e. Formalised Folklore. It is significant that in the discussions of folklore in Bengali Language in the North-Eastern region, Material Folklore has not been given due importance. Again in Formalised Folklore, most of the discussions have been centred on folk literature. Among the subjects that come under folk literature, proverbs and adages have been paid the largest amount of attention, though folksongs, riddles and rhymes have not been completely deprived of this. Comparatively little attention has been given to folk tales, folk rituals, folkart, folk language, folkdance, folk games and folk deities. And such subjects as Mantra literature, Magic cult, folk medicine, Fairs and Festivals have been left virtually unattended.

In the articles referred to, materials taken from folk literature have been primarily studied. It deserves pointing out that long narrative works of folk literature have not been collected. Again only the literary beauty of the materials has been analysed by the authors. At times they pointed out the liberal and secular aspects discernible in the materials. The backdrop of the compositions of the available materials, comparative study with other forms of literature and sociological analysis are almost absent.

A comparison between the articles written in the Pre-independence period and those written during the fifty years after independence will reveal that except in a few cases there has not been any significant qualitative advancement in the field. The modern analytical study of folklore in the Bengali language in the North-Eastern region was initiated through Padmanath Bhattacharjee's 'Srehatter Prabadbakya' published in 1915 in *Sreebhumi,* a monthly magazine published from Karimganj. In the said work Padmanath Bhattacharjee's emphasis was on collection of materials and discussion on literary beauty of the collected materials. The same tradition is being more or less followed even now. In respect of collection, only a fraction of the rich material of the folk literature of the North Eastern region has been collected. Only one example would make the position clear. As far back as in 1942 Rajmohan Nath collected a long ballad called *Sonadhaner Geet* from Jayanta region and published it in 1942. Although there are numerous other ballads current in the Southern part of Assam, nobody during more than half a century since then has collected any ballad or folklore and published the same.

The loopholes of the articles may be discerned from another angle of view. Credibility, which depends on amassing of evidence, is the fundamental condition of a research work. It is essential to point out the source of every collected material to establish credibility. Again, the reference to the source makes the works of the later researchers easier, for they may, depending upon the reference, verify the facts by visiting the field. It makes feasible the study whether there has been any change in the material caused by the passage of time. Many of the published articles show the lack of consciousness of the authors to these essentials.

Today every branch of knowledge is being enriched by newer ideas and application of newer methodology. In the field of folklore research the multidisciplinary approach is getting increasing importance. In the matter of analysis nothing new can be done without any initiation to modern theoretical speculations. In the articles written in Bengali language in the North-Eastern region on folk lore there is an obvious weakness in this sphere. This weakness has to be overcome for the sake of modern research.

Some important articles on folklore of North-East India written in Bengali language are being furnished below:

Ahamed Kamaluddin

(a) Baraker Sanskriti Chetanay Sitalang Shah, *Souvenir, Barak Upatyaka Banga Sahitya O Sanskriti Sammelan,* 12th Conference, 1398 B.E., Ed-Subir Kar, Karimganj.
(b) Barak Upatyakar Sanskritik Bikashe Upajatiya Prabhab, *Souvenir Barak Upatyaka Banga Sahitya O Sanskriti Sammelan,* 13th Conference, 1399 B.E., ED. Ratnasekhar Bhattacharjee, Lala.

Bari, Mahabubul

(a) Cacharer Lok Sahitya Prabad, A collection 357 Bengali Proverbs of Barak Valley with brief note have been published in weekly *Arunodoy* from 24th June 1976 to 16th June, 1977 issue. Ed. Sunil Dutta Roy, Silchar.
(b) Cacharer Gramanchale Bahul Prachalita Kayeti Krira Bisayak Chara, *Souvenir,* 6th Dist., Rural Sports Festival, 1977, Ed. Mahabubul Bari, Silchar.
(c) Cacharer Palli Sahitya, *Souvenir,* Cachar Banga Sahitya O Sanskriti Sammelan, 2nd Annual Conference, 1384 B.E., Ed. Partha Sarathi Chanda, Silchar.
(d) Barak Upatyakar Laukik Sanskar, Daily *Jugasankha,* 5th, 12th, 19th November issue, 1995. Ed. Atin Das, Silchar.

Basu, Sibtapan

(a) Jangiyar Gan, Daily *Samay Prabaha*, 5th January, 1996 issue, Ed. Sukumar Bagchi, Guwahati.
(b) Barak Upatyakar Lok Sanskriti Prasange, *Champakali*, Sarad Sankhya, 1403 B.E., Ed. Jashim Uddin Laskar, Algapur, Hailakandi Dist.
(c) Uttar Purba Bharater Krishibhittik Loknritya, Daily *Jugasanka*, 13th April issue, 1997.
(d) Baraker Anchalik Bangla Chara, *Chirantani*, The Annual journal of Karimganj Lok Sanskriti Parisad, 2nd issue, September, 1997, Karimganj.

Bhattacharjee, Amalendu

(a) Cachar jelar Swadeshi Lok Sangeet, *Amader Samakal*, 5th year 2nd & 3rd issue, November 1982, Ed. Hirendra Kumar Bhattacharjee, Silchar.
(b) Cachar Jelar Laukik Krira, *Souvenir*, North-East Inter College Badminton competition, Inaugural Number, 14th January, 1982, G.C. College, Silchar Ed. Sudip Choudhury.
(c) Yatra: Barak Upatyakay, *Lok Sanskriti Gabesana*, 7th year, 2nd issue, 1994, Lok Sanskriti Gabesana Parisad, Ed. Sanat Mitra, Calcutta.
(d) Barak Upatyakay Arya-Brahmanya Prabhaber Suchana : Kayekti Analocita O Lokayata Tathyasutra, *Gabesana Parisad Patrika*, First issue, Barak Upatyaka Banga Sahitya O Sanskriti Sammelan, 1996, Ed. Apurbananda Majumder, Silchar.

Bhattacharjee, Jayanta Bhusan

(a) Barak Upatyakar *Dak Sahitya*, Umium, 1992, Shillong.

Bhattacharjee, Kishore

(a) Prasanga: Assamer Lok Sanskriti, *Eka ebang Kayekjan*, 11th year, Sarat, 1397 B.E., Guwahati, Ed. Udayan Biswas.

Bhattacharjee, Mukundadas

(a) Cachar Jelar Ojha Nach, *Desh*, 31st year, 7th March 1964, Calcutta.

Chakraborty, Ajit Kumar

(a) Sreehatter Lok Charay Samajchitra, *Sreehatta Cacharer Prachin Itihas O Sanskriti Ruprekha*, Ed. Jyotirindranath Choudhury, Sunirmal Dutta Choudhury, Amalendu Bhattacharjee, Manabendra Bhattacharjee, Bangiya Sahitya Parisad, Shillong, 1996.
(b) Aitihyamay Sreehatta O Tar Lok Sanskritite Prabad, *Sreehatta Cacharer Prachin Itihas O Sanskritir Ruprekha*, Shillong.

Choudhury, Badarujjaman

(a) Barak Upatyakar Gramjivan O Gramin Sahitya: Aitiyer Uttaradhikar, *Souvenir*, Barak Upatyaka Banga Sahitya O Sanskriti Sammelan, 11th Conference, 1397 B.E., Ed. Apurbananda Majumder, Silchar.

Choudhury, Jyotirindranath

(a) Baul Kavi Radharaman, *Sreehatta Cacharer Prachin Itihas O Sanskritir Ruprekha*.

Choudhury, Sujit

(a) Vidyapatir Byaribhakti Tarangini, *Sahitya Parisat Patrika*, 87th year 2nd issue, Sravan-Aswin, 1387 B.E. Bangiya Sahitya Parisad, Calcutta.

Das, Monojit

(a) Sreehatta Cacharer Ekti Krishiparva; Bhuijura, Weekly *Dristipat*, Deepavali Sankhya, 1981, Ed, Bhupendra Kumar Singha, Karimganj.

(b) *Prasanga Paus Sankranti*, 16th Publication, Digboloy, 1395 B.E. Ed. Kamaluddin Ahamed, Kanishail, Karimganj.
(c) Barak Upatyakar Prabad Prabachene Samaj Jiban, *Souvenir*, Barak Upatyaka Banga Sahitya O Sanskriti Sammelan, 12th Annual Conference, 1398 B.E., Ed. Subir Kar, Karimganj.
(d) Barak Upatyakay Pracgilita Dhadha ba heyali, Kha, 1st, 2nd & 3rd Joint issue, 1398-99 B.E. Ed. Jamuna Choudhury & Alekhya Bhattacharjee, Karimganj.

Das, Nisith Ranjan

(a) Barak Upatyakar Prabad Prabachan, *Kalpurus*, Annual Number, 1994, Ed. Jahar Jyoti Chakraborty, Katirail, Karimganj.
(b) Barak Upatyakar Laukik Bhasar Abhidhan, *Akshar Britta*, 4th year, 2nd issue, April, 1994, Ed. Kapish Kanti Dey, Karimganj.
(c) Barak Upatyakar Sthan namer baisisthya, *Akshar Britta*, 6th year, 4th issue, August 1996.

Deb, Shankar

(a) Faguyar Kathigan, *Udharband, Saradiya Sankhya*, 1994, Ed. Sankar Deb, Udharband.

Demta, Kajal

(a) Tusugan: Barak Upatyakar Cha-bagan Sramikder Sukh duhkher Rojnamcha, *Souvenir, Barak Upatyaka Banga Sahitya O Sanskriti Sammelan, 8th Conference*, 1393 B.E., Khaspur.

Kar, Subir

(a) Uttar Purba Bharater Lok Sahitya Bidraha Chetana, *Souvenir*, published on the occasion of the 5th year of Charanik, 1995, Karimganj.

Majumdar, Abul Hussain

(a) Hachan Raja O Tar Ganer Darshan O Adhyatmabad, *Sreehatta Cacharer Prachin Itihas O Sanskritir Ruprekha.*

Majumdar, Dibajyoti

(a) Samaj Vigyaner Nirikhe Ekti Lok Katha, *Sangvarta,* 1st issue, Book Fair 1994, Ed. Dhruba Kumar Mukhapadhaya, Howrah, West Bengal.

Nath, Ashish Ranjan

(a) Barak Upatyakar Lok Sanskritir Ek Samriddha Dik, Dhamail, Dainik *Jugasankha,* 13th July 1995.

Nath, Tushar Kanti

(a) Sibrai Gamadi Upasana : Dimacha Sanskritir Ekti Dik, *Souvenir,* Barak Upatyaka Banga Sahitya O Sanskriti Sammelan, 12th Annual Conference, 1398 B.E.
(b) Dimacha Lok Sahitya: Busu Gan Prasanga, Digboloy, Magh-Chaitra, 1399 B.E.
(c) Karbi Lok Sahitya: Sasya Bandana Prasanga, *Gana Arsi,* Nov-Dec, 1992, Ed. Mahuya Choudhury, Silchar.
(d) Kukur: Asamer Upajatiya Sanskritite, *Lok Sanskriti Gabesana,* Vol.10, No.2, 1997, Calcutta.

Purkait, Nikhilesh

(a) Asamer Goalparay Prachilita Manasar Gan, *Journal of the Department of Bengali,* Guwahati University, 1995-96, Academic year, Guwahati.

Roy, Mahindra

(a) Surma Barak Upatyakar Prabachan, *Sambhar,* Sarad Sankhya, 15th year, 1381 B.E. Ed. Manatosh Chakraborty, Silchar.

Sen, Gouri

(a) Sreehatter Meyeli Bratacharer Utsa Sandhane, *Sreehatta Cacharer Prachin Itihas O Sanskritir Ruprekha*, Shillong, 1996.

Sen, Soumen

(a) Khasi Rupkathar Pratirup, *Sanskriti,* Rabindra Smriti Granthagar, 1992, Ed. Shankar Chakraborty, Shillong.

Chapter V

STATUS OF GARO LANGUAGE

M.S. Sangma

Ethnically and linguistically, the Garos belong to a group of languages called by Brian Hodgson as 'Bodo'. The Bodos comprised of the Bara-kachari Garo, Dimasa, Rabha, Mech, Lalung, Koch, Chutiya, Reang, Kokborok, etc., who spread over the whole of the Brahmaputra valley, Tripura and Bengal including Bangladesh, forming a solid block in North-East India as one of the main bases of the present day population. The Bodo, in turn, is a section of the Tibeto-Burman speech family which comprises a series of dialects spoken from Tibet in the north to Myanmar in the south and from Baltistan in the west to Chinese Provinces of Szechuan and Yunnan in the east. The Tibeto-Burman family is one of the main branches of the Sino-Tibetan speech family and the area of the characterisation of the primitive Tibeto-Chinese speech has been found to be in the north-western China between the headwaters of Hoangho and Yang-tse-Kiang rivers.[1]

The language spoken by the Garos is called as "A'chik Ku'sik" by the Garos of India and "Mande Ku'sik" by the Garos of Bangladesh. "A'chik Ku'sik" literally means the language of hillman, whereas, "Mande Ku'sik" means the language of man.[2] Today, Tura is looked up as the literary centre of the Garo language by all the Garos living in different parts of North-East India, as far as West Bengal including Bangladesh.

Like other languages, the Garo language has a number of dialects, which bear strong resemblance with one another, though to an outsider, the differences may be striking enough. In olden days, each dialectic group settled in isolation, had no or very little contact with others. In effect, they evolved not only different dialects but also varied cultural traits. The A'we dialect, the Chisak, Dual, Matchi, Matjangchi, A'beng, Chibok, Ruga, Gara-Ganching, Atong, Megam, etc., are the main dialects with sub-dialects that exist in Bangladesh only, such as, Braks, Jariadong, Somons, Galnes and Malongs.[3] However, all these dialects are fast disappearing today due to the adoption of the A'we dialect as the language of Garo literature and medium of instruction in all educational institutions, which in effect, has become also the *lingua franca* of the Garos.

Oral and Traditional Literature

The Garos have a rich vocabulary. This rich heritage has been preserved by them in the form of oral conversations, narration of stories and jokes, chanting of traditional sacrificial rites and incantations, folk songs, proverbs and maxims, historical narrations, wailings, etc. Unfortunately, many of these oral traditions have not yet been gleaned and compiled and are fast disappearing due to modernisation processes.

Written Literature

The Garos do not have a literary tradition, nor do they have a script of their own, though they have a tradition that they had their written literature on rolls of parchment of animals which they had eaten it up by boiling at the time of starvation while they were still at Mandalay in Myanmar.[4]

The Garo words were first reduced to writing by the British Officials and the American Baptist Missionaries in Roman script which were published in different issues of the *Journal of the Asiatic Society of Bengal*. Therefore, the first Garo literature was in the form of compilation of Garo words with the equivalent words of cognate tribes and English. The Garo vocabulary was first compiled by John Elliott, Commissioner of Dacca, and was published in the Third Volume of *Asiatic Researches in 1799*[5] which was followed by others.

The next stage in the development of Garo literature was the publication of a few Primers and Readers for the Lower Primary schools as well as a some Christian literature published both in Roman and Bengali characters. This was followed by the publication of books on Garo Grammar though elementary in nature.

The shifting of the American Baptist headquarters from Goalpara to Tura in 1878 witnessed the concentration of efforts of the Missionaries as well as a few local literates in the work of translation of the whole Bible, which was brought to a successful conclusion by 1924. In order to step up their efforts for creating religious environment, the Missionaries with the help of local literates, translated into Garo a few religious books such as, *Pilgrim's Progress, Mirror of the Heart, The Peep of Day, Catechisms, Sunday School Lessons, Stories from the Bible* and the monthly magazine called *A'chikni Ripeng or the Friends of the Garos,* etc. Thus Christian themes dominated the Garo literature till about 1940.

Secular literature began among the Garos only after 1940s with the publication of the Garo magazine entitled *A'chik Ku'rang* or the *Voice of the Garos* by a few Garos who studied in the Cotton College at Guwahati under the able leadership of Prof. Howard Denison W. Momin, then Lecturer of English in Cotton College, Guwahati. From around 1940s till today, the Garos produced the greatest number of Garo literature in different forms some of which were either translated or adapted while some others were original.

Dictionary

1. The first compilation of Garo words was made by John Elliott, Commissioner of Dacca, with English renderings which was published in 1799. Second compilation of Garo words was by Francis Hamilton and contained a comparative vocabulary of about 1800 words in English and other languages of cognate tribes. Third attempt was by Rev. Nathan Brown in 1837 and then by William Robinson in 1849, Hodgson in 1849, Ramnath

Chakravarty in 1867, Williamson in 1869 and others. All these were printed in *JASB*, Calcutta.

2. The first Bengali-Garo Dictionary was prepared by Rev. Ramke W. Momin, which contained more than thirty-five thousand words and was published by the American Baptist Mission in 1887. This was, however, reprinted in Roman script in 1996.
3. The third Dictionary was by Rev. M.C. Mason, English-Garo in 1920, Calcutta.
4. Next was by D.S. Nengminsa called *Garo-English Dictionary*, 1940.
5. D.S. Nengminsa published again *Garo-English Dictionary* in 1954.
6. In 1955, K.W. Momin published *English-Achikku Dictionary* in Calcutta.
7. Next was *English-Garo Dictionary* by Rangam G. Momin in 1957.
8. Another outstanding work in this field was the *Garo-Garo-English-Assamese Dictionary* by H.W. Marak published by the Assam Academy for Cultural Relations in 1975.
9. A group of Garos compiled *Oxford Picture Dictionary* which was published by Oxford Press, Calcutta, 1978.
10. The latest publication was *A'chikku-English Dictionary* by Miss L.M. Holbrook and was published by the Garo Literature Society in 1998.

Out of the publications mentioned above, *Garo-Garo-English-Assamese Dictionary* by H.W. Marak contains 14,778 Garo words, while *A'chikku-English Dictionary* by Holbrook contains 14,287 Garo words, and so, they are the best ones so far.

Grammar

Books on Garo Grammar are still few and far between. Whatever Grammar books have been published are still at the school level.

1. The first attempt to write Garo Grammar in English was made by William Robinson, an Educational Officer in

Assam in 1849, which was published in *JASB*, Vol. XVII, 1849, Calcutta.

2. The second book on Garo Grammar was prepared and published by Rev. Miles Bronson in 1868.
3. The third book on Garo Grammar was prepared and published by Rev. F.J. Keith, an American Baptist Missionary stationed at Goalpara in 1874.

All these works were elementary in nature and were intended to introduce the Garo language and its Grammar to the British Government as a part of their ongoing studies and research of unknown tribes.

4. The next book on Garo Grammar was prepared and published by Rev. E.G. Phillips, an American Baptist Missionary, stationed at Tura in 1904, as a textbook for the Garo schools. This book has been reprinted several times and is still used as a textbook in schools.
5. R.G. Momin prepared and published *English Grammar and Composition*, Calcutta, 1939, which was used by High School students.
6. D.S. Nengminsa also published *English Grammar and Translation*, Calcutta, 1957, which served the needs of the students.
7. Samson K. Sangma also published *Achik Grammar*, Calcutta, 1970, which was intended for the beginners.
8. Clearshon K. Sangma published *Primary School Grammar and Translation*, Gauhati, 1983.
9. Robins Burling, Professor of Anthropology, Michigan University, USA, prepared *A Garo Grammar*. It was published by the Deccan College, Pune, 1961. This book is highly technical and is very useful for the understanding of the Garo language.

Christian Literature

Translation of the *Bible* into Garo language received the attention of the American Baptist Missionaries first who took fifty years 1874–1924 in the translation of the whole *Bible*.

Their next works were the printing of Catechisms and Garo hymnals, both translated and composed. Other works on Garo Christian literature were Miss Mason's *The Peep of Day*, 1888; E.G. Phillips, *Christ the Lord, Pastor's Handbook*, 1891, *First Introductions on Religion*, 1893, and *The Way to Health* by Bakal Sangma; *Calling Attention to Mission Work* by Thangkan Sangma, 1895; *Boggs Tonic Solfa Tune Book*, Phillips *The Mirror of the Heart* 1896, *Our Duty*, 1902, and *The Basic Tenets of Christ*, 1904, and *The Sunday School Lessons*, 1909, and *Fellowship with Christ* by Dr. Crozier, 1910. Rev. Mason also prepared and published *The Origin of the Church and the Work of the Apostles*, 1912.

Other varieties of Christian literature are *The Stories from the Bible*, 1932; Fr. Pianazzi's *Sing to the Lord*, 1935, and three of Miss Holbrook's publications, namely, *Bought by Blood*, 1936, *The Hebrews*, 1938, and *Sastroni Katarang* or the stories from the Old Testament, 1939. But the most notable works at this time were the translation of the *Pilgrim's Progress* into Garo language by Wilson K. Marak in 1936, and *A Compendium of fifty tracts* prepared and printed by F.W. Harding, which forms the basis of Baptist Faith, Beliefs and Practices, 1940.

In 1966, Garo Baptist Book Club was formed under the general editorship of Rev. James M. Wood. The following books have been translated and published by this Club—

1. *Ka'donge Baltigipa* (The Brave Messenger) by W.K. marak, 1966.
2. *Nangni Songsulna Ka'sabo* (Love your neighbour) by G.K. Marak, 1967.
3. *Isolaro Mande* (God and Man) by K.D. Sangma, 1968.
4. *Matini gimin Seani* (St. Matthew) by P.S. Momin, 1969.

The Club became disfunctional after the departure of Rev. James N. Wood. Yet its publications made great contributions to the Garo literature.

The Roman Catholic Church which began their mission work from Tura in 1932, also devoted a large part of their time to the preparation and publication of Christian literature. Fr. Pianazzi who was one of the two founder Fathers of the Catholic Mission in Garo Hills was a pioneer in this respect. He not only made extensive tours in the hills but also made extensive writings on various aspects of the Catholic Mission. Out of his many publications of books, booklets and Tracts, *The History of the Catholic Church*, Vol. I, 1945 and Vol. II, 1958, and *Sing to the Lord*, 1955, which was a collection of 50 hymns in Garo language are remarkable.

Father G. Costa, an anthropologist, and a writer of international repute, wrote and published *Sacraments of the Catholics*, 1950.

Of late, two Fathers stand out as eminent writers among them. They are Fr. Mankin who published a large number of books and booklets, out of which, *Janggini Rama* or the Path of the Soul, 1980, and *Life of Christ*, 1981, may be mentioned. But the most prolific writer was Father Anthony Buccieri who published about 15 books and a number of booklets and pamphlets, of which, mention may be made of the translation of the Latin work, *Immitation of Christ*, 1989; *Pinokkini*, 1994, Italian stories for children, and the life of *Joan of Arc*, 1996.

Other Mission Societies, such as, the Seventh Day Adventist and the Christian Literature Centre also added to the volumes of Garo Christian Literature by publishing booklets and pamphlets.

Folktales

The Garos possess a variety of folktales, which the fathers used to tell their children before they go to sleep at night. But the British officials and the Missionaries having no interest in them, it was left to the local literates to glean and publish them. Thus, it was Simison R. Sangma and Jobang D. Marak who collected about 15 such folktales and published them in 1927, for the first time. This work was then taken up by Dhoronsing Sangma who published them in three volumes containing 145 tales, Vol. I in 1939, Vol. II in 1956, and Vol. III in 1963. Harendra W. Marak was another compiler of Garo folktales who collected about 42 tales and published them in 1957. All these stories were simple folktales like that of Aesop's Fables, some of which deal with the following –

> The Frog and the Monkey, The Elephant and an Ant, Two Sisters who Slept in the Jhum Hut, The Firefly and the Monkey, The Peacock's Neck, The Elephant and the Porcupine, The Jackal, The Ghost, The Goat, The Crab, The Monkey and the Tortoise, The Dove, The Man called Tengton, etc.

Dewansing Rongmuthu made a notable contribution towards the understanding of the rich cultural heritage of the Garos by his collections and publications. The first of these was *Apasong Agana* or As told by forefathers, 1970, which contained the traditional stories of their origin, migrations, settlements and the origin of things. His second work was in English entitled *The Folktales of the Garos*, 1960. His other books on folktales and folklore are *The Epic Lore of the Garos*, 1967; *Jadoreng or the Psycho-Physical Culture of the Garos*, 1993, and *The Traditional Dances of the Garos*, 1996. Thus, he made the most extensive researches and publications on this aspect of the life of the people.

Despite the works mentioned above, there is still much more work to be done.

Poetry

Of all aspects of Garo literature, it was in the field of poetry that the Garos made the biggest stride. They are lovers of songs and music and they sang as they danced and composed as they sang. This was done in the case of *Katha Agana* or Epic narration or in the case of any song sung during jhum festival.

When Christianity was introduced, few Garo literates along with the Missionaries directed their attention to the composition of hymns, some of which are still sung today. When education was introduced, generally people tended to write poems rather than fiction, though quality is another thing. However, a large number of poems have been published ranging from war and peace, love and hatred, patriotic and romantic, philosophical and historical, on nature and seasons, rural and urban life, etc.

Mention may be made of Prof. Howard Denison Momin's poems, such as, "The Voice of the Garos", "You will be Remembered", "The New Year", and "The Woman and the Tobacco"; and Karnesh Marak's "Inheritance"; Evelyn Marak's "The Rose", "For You", "Oh My Garo Land", and Mrs. Jonmoni Shira's "When", "Daisy", "The World a Nightmare", etc. These poems compare well with poems of any other language.

Drama

There are altogether 17 plays so far in Garo language. Some of them such as, *Nokdang* (The Family) by K.M. Momin, *Kamni Bite* (Fruit of one's action) by A.G. Momin, *Sin'kari* (Winter) by C.R. Marak, *Skul Master* by L.D. Shira depict the socio-economic conditions of the time, whereas some of them are based on historical figures, such as, *Togan, the Warrior* by H.N. Sangma and L.R. Marak is based on the historical figure. *Muga Dingsepa* by K.R. Marak, *Dikki* by L.R. Marak, *Serejing-Waljan and Aje and Gilje* are based on the Garo legendary figures and the two plays by K.R. Marak, namely, *Macbeth* is an adaptation from Shakespeare's *Macbeth and Veniceni Badinggina* is a translation of Shakespeare's *The Merchant of Venice.*

Stories

Apart from folktales, there are also stories published by some authors some of which are based on the traditional stories, some centre round the legendary figures and some of them are either created or adapted from stories of other lands.

Proverbs and Phrases

Proverbs and Phrases were so long in the memory of the people. But of late, six publications have come out. Out of them the publications by M.S. Sangma and J.R.L. Marak contain the highest number coming to 1004. Garo Phrases also reached 300 mark. However, as we go round different parts of Garo Hills, more and more of them are still being discovered.

Novel

Only five novels have been produced so far. Out of them, Mrs. I.R. Marak's *Chigitchakgreni Nokma* (The Chief of Chikitchakgre), 1984, and *Gamseng* are her own creation and style, whereas, *Khalsin* and *Sonachi* by Redin Momin is based on the legendary story and Simieon R. Sangma's *Sonobal Me'chik* is an adaptation from a Bengali Novel and M. Rongmuthu's *Mama Tomni Jandap* is a translation from English.

Works in Translation

Works in translation form an important element in the development of Garo literature. When the schools were started in Garo Hills, most of the textbooks for schools were either translated or adapted from English books. Thus, with the passing of time, a number of books both from English and Bengali have been translated into Garo language of which, the most important Works are listed below –

Wilson K. Marak translated and published *Pilgrim's Progress, Selected Stories and Poems from Tagore, Sadhu Sundar Singh, The Burning of Rome City,Christ will come Again, The Brave Messenger, The Arabian Nights and Stories from Shakespeare* by Charles Lamb.

Mackenson Rongmuthu translated and published Shakespeare's *The Merchant of Vanice and The Winter's Tale.* Mrs. Bimolin Momin translated and published some famous stories like *Ulysses, Helen of Troy,* etc.; K.M. Momin translated and published *Benhur,* Redin Momin *Ramayana* and Dr. S. Marak, *Mahabharata.*

Garo Literary Criticism

Books on this aspect of literature are still in an initial stage. Only with the introduction of Honours and Post-Graduate Courses in Garo three or four books have been published out of compulsion on literary criticism. They are *Elements of Literary Criticism* by M.S. Sangma, *Gisik Matgrikrang* by L.D. Shira, *Rhetoric and Prosody* by V.S. Sangma and *Garo Literary Criticism* by L.D. Shira.

History

Books on history also have not yet reached a high standard. There are books on the History of the Garos by Josang D. Marak, Levisond N. Sangma, Mihir N. Sangma and Moniram R. Marak. There are also books on the History of Assam and India and the History of Meghalaya State. Standard books are still wanting.

Biography

There are altogether ten biographies and one autobiography. Rev. K.D. Sangma has written and published biographies of *Eisenhower* and *John F. Kennedy* and W.K. Marak on the life of *Sadhu Sundar Singh*. K.W. Momin wrote the biography of *Rev. Ramke Momin* and Surendra Marak on the life of three prominent Garo leaders. Mihir N. Sangma has written the biography of *Capt. Williamson A. Sangma,* the first Chief Minister of Meghalaya State, and M.S. Sangma has published a short biography of *Sonaram R. Sangma,* the first Garo politician.

From what has been described above, it is clear that the Garo literature in any aspect has not yet reached a high standard. Though the Garo language was first reduced to writing and publication in 1799, in the *Asiatic Researches,* Vol. III, Calcutta, and thus, is now two hundred years old, yet the growth and development of Garo literature has been very slow. It is hoped that with the introduction of M.A. Course in Garo, it will take more rapid strides first in literature and then in social sciences and humanities.

References

1. G.A. Grierson, *Linguistic Survey of India,* Vol. III, Part I.
2. *Ibid.,* Vol. I, part I, Introduction.
3. *Ibid.*
4. D.S. Rongmuthu, *Folktales of the Garos,* pp. 1–2.
5. John Elliott, *Asiatic Researches,* Vol. III, Calcutta, 1799.

Chapter VI

STATUS OF HISTORICAL WRITING IN KHASI

D.R. Syiemlieh

I

In the select bibliography in English and Khasi of Hamlet Bareh's *The History and Culture of the Khasi People*, the author notes that uptill 1967-68, "nothing on the history and culture of the Khasis came out. Thereupon my effort to produce it"[1]. It may be true that nothing substantial and comprehensive had been written in English, though his interpretation of events and processes had to depend on existing published histories. A close look at his Khasi sources and a search for what had preceded and came after this first comprehensive history of the Khasis reveals a fair interest among the community in their history, the nation and even world events. That the Khasis had a sense of history is reflected in their oral tradition and folklore. That today these traditions are being lost out with the many influences on the Khasi society and the lack of appreciation of how the Khasis came to be till the present, is sadly reflected in their lack of interest in the past. In this context the seminar on "Status of Social Sciences in Vernacular Languages in North East India" assumes significance as this would be among the first to attempt to examine the literature that has been generated in the various vernacular languages in the region. This paper will examine the histories that have been written in Khasi and situate the status of the subject both as an academic discipline and matter of historical interest.

II

Much after Rev. Thomas Jones started the use in 1842 of Roman Script for the Khasi language was history written. In the first flush of literary works a combination of primers, Christian literature and translations were published. Beginning with a translation of *Rhodd Mam* (1842), a popular Welsh story, Jones worked on *Ca Citap Nyngkong Ban Hicai Poole Ci Citin Cassi* (First Khasi Reader, (1842), *Oo Nonghicai* (*The Instructor*, 1843), and *Ca Gospel Jong OO Mathiaos*, 1847). By the time Rev. William Lewis tried his hand in the new expression some standardisation had taken place. He added a small catechism, a hymn book (1850) and a translation of the Four Gospels and the Acts of the Apostles (1856).[2] In 1855, Rev William Pryse's *Khasi Grammar* was published. In the Prefatory Note to the vocabulary, Pryse takes a stand that the Khasis, "a small and uninfluential tribe will not be able to retain characters different from those of the larger natives of the plains which surround their hills." He continued:[3]

> Should the Khasia tribe be ever brought under the influence of education, civilisation, and commercial intercourse, the Bengali character must supplant the Roman at a not very distant day.

Pryse may have been influenced in this opinion as he had started work among the Bengalis of Sylhet. Perhaps a not too encouraging start of the three schools at Mawmluh, Mawsmai and Cherrapunji where Khasi was taught and the British Official policy of encouraging the use of the Bengali script,[4] had Pryse write these lines. The debate of which script to use was not a long one. By the 1860's-1870's the decision of the Welsh Mission to use the Roman Script prevailed.[5] It was followed by an outpouring of literature that stimulated literary creativity in prose, poetry and drama; the establishment of Ri Khasi Press (1896) and monthly journals *U Khasi Mynta* (1896), *U Nongphira* (1903), *Nongkit Khubor* (1889), replaced in 1902 by *U Nongialam Kristan*. It was not long before Calcutta

University, where many Khasis first went for higher education, gave recognition of the development of the language in its many expressions when it decided in 1902 that Khasi could be included in the use of subjects for the Entrance Examination.[6]

III

Before and by the turn of the century fragments of Khasi history were appearing in Alexander Mackenzie, *History of the Relations of the Government with the Tribes of the North East Frontier of Bengal* (1884); W.W. Hunter, *A Statistical Account of Assam* (1879); C.U. Aitchison, *A Collection of Treatise, Engagements and Sanads* (1892), (1909); J.H. Morris, *The History of the Welsh Calvinistic Methodists' Foreign Mission* (1910), and D. Herbert, *Report on Succession to Siemships in the Khasi Hills* (1902). These and other material in the *Journal of the Asiatic Soceity of Bengal*, reprints of A.J.M. Mills, *Report on the Khasi and Jaintia Hills 1853* (1901), and W.J. Allen, *Report on the Administration on Cossyah and Jynteah Hill Territory, 1858* (1903), would have enabled B.K. Sarma-Roy to write *Ka Histori Jong Ka Ri Khasi*, Shillong, 1914. The book of 104 pages has chapters on the Khasi states, a chapter on neighbouring Manipur and one on the Syiemlieh clan.[7] From the title of this first history in Khasi, its subject was the Khasi people. As an observer of the society B.K. Sarma-Roy's work becomes important as a reference point. When Homiwell Lyngdoh published his *magnum opus, Ki Syiem Khasi Bad Synteng*, Shillong, 1938, he does not refer to the history mentioned above. He has as a reference Joel Gatphoh's *Ka Histori Ki Syiem Synteng Ha Ka Jingshisha* (1923–1926) which unfortunately is not located. Lyngdoh's book was a trend setter for historical studies in Khasi. He goes into a long introduction of the origin of Syiemship, its variations, powers and functions of Syiems, the role of the founding clans *Bakhraw*, the Khasi religion linked with the Khasi *Himas*. Then follow nineteen chapters in which accounts are given of 18 Syiemships. The start given with this has made the study of the Khasi Himas in general a recurring theme in Khasi histories, of which more will be said shortly.

It must have been rather difficult for Khasis to write histories in the vernacular during the closing years of British control over them. Homiwell did not closely examine the effects British paramountcy was having over the institution of Syiemship. Rather he is impressed that some of the Syiems had titles of "Rai Bahadur", "Raja", the M.B.E. and O.B.E. conferred on them. Though Rev. J.J.M. Nichols-Roy did not write a history, many of his writings with their political bend made use of history. We may here cite just one of his pamphlets: *Ka Ri Khasi Bad Jaintia: Shabar Bad Hapoh Ka Reform*. The lecture was distributed in October 1936 to educate the Khasis of their position in the reformed constitution of 1935. He would continue to write till the 1950s both in Khasi and English on a variety of subjects.[8]

With independence came the freedom to interpret the history of Khasi-Jaintia. In this new approach L.L.D. Basan very early published a bilingual pamphlet *The Khasi States under the Indian Union*, (1948), which questioned the position of the Khasis under the Indian Union and the process by which the Khasi states and British villages had come into an Assam administration. Many years were to pass before L.G. Shullai took up where L.L.D. Basan left. Over the years Shullai has almost single-handedly campaigned for another look into the status of the Khasi Syiem, the integration of the Khasi Jaintia Hills into the Indian Union and kindred other topics. His *Ki Hima Khasi* (1975) draws much from the references noted above and from the author's perserverance in collecting every scrap of information on the subject of the Khasi Syiems. The importance of this small book is that it updates the issue to the present times and has become a ready reference on the Khasi Syiems. A variation of this appeared not long after in *Ka Ri Shnong Pdeng Pyrthei* (1978), the introduction of which is addressed to the youth as an inspiration for them to see their society as distinct despite their small numbers. Other writings of L.G. Shullai that have a historical approach are *Ki Symboh History Bad Ka Ri Hynniewtrep* (1989), a collection of essays on aspects of British rule in India; the Assam Legislature 1912-1950, the Constituent Assembly of India, and the administration of the Khasi-Jaintia Hills after 1950 and till 1974. Rather disappointing was the contents of I. Nongbri's

Ka History Ka Ri Hynniewtrep (1992), but a close look at the cover clears that the history he writes, starts in 1952. His is a repetition of what Shullai and Basan had earlier published; more particularly in the appendices that form a large part of the paperback. To his credit are the appendices of interesting letters of Wickliffe Syiem of Nongstoin.

IV

Before we again bring the history down to our times it would be convenient to go back to the early part of the century and again build up the literature on other aspects of history. In the face of the spread of Christianity in the hills and the establishment of the Seng Khasi (1899) Jeebon Roy wrote *Ka Niam Jong Ki Khasi* (1897); Radhon Singh Berry published *Ka Jingsneng Tymmen Shaphang Ka Akor Khasi* (1902) and Rabon Singh Kharsuka authored a book *Ka Kitab Jingphawar* (1905). These stalwarts of Khasi religion and culture are especially noted for they gave the Khasi society a strong influence to remain in the traditional faith. A church elder in Homiwell Lyngdoh, with his strong sense of history wrote a study of the cremation rites of the Sohra Syiems and the rituals of the Shad Nongkrem at Smit.[9] To this he added in 1937, *Ka Niam Khasi*. In it he centres on the basic ideas of the Khasi faith, depicting its religious performances, the chanting of prayers, incantations and ceremonies relating to different social occasions. Just how concerned he and others were about the past is illustrated in the studies by two Salesian priests. J. Bachhiarello could identify himself with the people sufficiently to author *Ki Dienjat Ki Longshuwa* (1930). Another of his confreres G. Costa endeared himself to the Khasis with his *Ka Riti Jong Ki Laiphew Syiem* (1936). These writings in Khasi have become invaluable texts for scholars wishing to pursue a search into the Khasi past. While at this stage of Khasi religion, it would not be inappropriate to note the histories of Christianity. A *Centenary History Ka Balang Presbyterian* was published in 1941. Though many small tracts had been brought out by that time it was only in 1966 that Rev. G. Angell Jones translated and updated J.H. Morris' history. The Catholic mission history is best done by Fr. O. Paviotti, *Ka Matti Jong U* (1989). Fr

H.Elias', *Ka Histori Jong Ka Balang Catholic* (1965) and Francis Diengdoh's *Ka History Jong Ka Balang* (1980) give a general picture of the Catholic Church's history.

It is not intended to exclude a history of Khasi poetry, prose and drama for these were as important in the transformation of the Khasis as other factors such as education, British administration and urbanization. As much has already been done on this by the members of the Khasi Author's Society it may suffice to note that the Khasi literature has grown sufficiently to be reflective of a society's wish that their language and literature receive the recognition of the Sahitya Academy.

Today a trend is clearly emerging in Khasi history of biography sketches and monographs. Tirot Singh and Kiang Nangbah two resistance leaders have received a fair amount of adulation and if the present position is any indication, the lives of these patriots will continue to inspire writers.[10] Thomas Jones is beginning to find a more befitting place in Khasi history.[11] J.J.M. Nichols Roy has found his biographer in O.L. Snaitang.[12] Dr John Roberts a medical missionary is given a sketch by L.G. Shullai.[13] Other Khasis such as Jeebon Roy, Mavis Dunn Lyngdoh already have accounts of them in English and it may be not before long that Khasi readers are made familiar with their lives. The most recent biography is on Wickliffe Syiem.[14]

V

In the absence of comprehensive histories one has to be on the watch for small pamphlets, booklets and paperbacks such as V.B. Ryngnga's, *Na Them Riwar* (1992), a collection of 20 short notices in the War area. Short histories of the Khasi *Himas* are not many. One such is E.W. Chyne's, *Ka History Jong Ka Hima Mawlong* (1977) which is a useful little booklet. Another small publication is Jor Manick Syiem's *Ka Jingiathuh Khana Shaphang Ki Syiem Jong Ka Hima Mylliem 1830–1960* (1984). Spiton Kharakor's, *Ki Khun Ki Ksiew U Hynniew Trep* (1981) makes very interesting reading, particularly the chapters Ki Kur U Hynniew Trep and Ki Jait U Hynniew Trep which enumerates 3363 Khasi clans. Other essays are on a variety of subjects relating to culture, Kiang Nangbah, Tirot Sing and the Khasi Natural Durbar.

One reason why history in Khasi has not acquired interest as much as literature has, is due to the absence of history in the vernacular in the school syllabus. An earlier generation of Khasi school goers had to go through texts[15] in Khasi, that made them familiar with the history of India and the world. For young students not familiar with English, this medium would have enabled them to better understand their histories. Today in the change of school syllabus history has taken a back seat. Whatever incentive was there to write history school texts is gone and so has the base for an appreciation of the past.

Another point to note is that the histories in the Khasi vernacular may have been written with the intention of portraying the past but many of the authors are not trained in the art of collecting, interpreting and presenting their findings. This has made the better written history rare. The Khasi historians, if we may make a categorisation have preferred the English medium for a number of reasons of which the principal would be that English would have a larger number of readers. Before long it is hoped the Khasis who are becoming increasingly conscious of their roots and culture will find histories relevant to this time and age.

References

1. H. Bareh, *The History and Culture of the Khasi People*, revised and enlarged edition, Shillong, 1985, p. 400.
2. Anon, "The Role of the Presbyterian Church in the Development of Khasi Language and Literature 1841-1902" in *Khasi Authors' Society: Souvenir 1842-1992*, pp. 12-13.
3. Cited by I.M. Simon, "A Tribute to the Rev. Thomas Jones", in *Ibid.*, pp. 25-26.
4. D.R. Syiemlieh, "Education, Elite and Politicisation in the Khasi-Jaintia Hills", in Ashish Bose *et al.* (ed.), *Tribal Demography and Development in North East India*, New Delhi, 1990, p.178.
5. D.R. Syiemlieh, *British Administration in Meghalaya: Policy and Pattern*, New Delhi, 1989, p.?
6. *Assam Administration Report 1902-1903*, p.44.
7. Cited in L.S. Gassah, "Don Katno Tylli Ki Elaka ha Ri Jaintia", in *Hynniewtrep Endeavour Society*, September 1989; and Suniti Kumar Chatterjee, *Kirata-Jana-Krti*, Calcutta, 1974, p. 172.

8. For a collection of J.J.M. Nichols-Roy's Writings see O.L. Snaitang, *Memoirs of Life and Political Writings of the Hon'ble Rev J.J.M. Nichols-Roy*, Shillong, 1998.
9. *Ka Pomblang bad Thang Syiem Sohra*, Shillong, 1928.
10. See H. Bareh, "Ka Thma Synteng Bad U Kiang Nongbah" (1961); *U Syiem Tirot Singh bad Kiwei Ki Para Syiem Ki Hima Khasi (1977); Shispah Sanphew Snew Mynshwa: U Tirot Singh bad Ka Mynnor ba Iphuh Iphieng* (1984); Quotient Sumer, *U Kiang Nangbah* (1978), and many Souvenirs released on the occasions of commemorating these leaders.
11. See the articles in *Khasi Authors' Society Souvenir 1842-1992* as an indication of this interest. Also S.S. Majaw, *U Kpa Ka Thoh Ka Tar Khasi*, Shillong, 1992.
12. O.L. Snaitang, *Ka Biography U Rev. J.J.M. Nichols-Roy*, Shillong, 1993.
13. L.G. Shullai, *U Dr John Roberts D.D.*, Shillong, 1975.
14. E.P. Syiem, *U Wickliffe Syiem Bad Ka Hima Nongstoin*, Nongstoin, 1998.
15. Prescribed for schools were Frank Pugh, *Ka Histori Jong Ka Khasi Jaintia Bad Assam*, Shillong (n.d.) and Tngensi Rynjah, *Ka History Ka Ri Khasi Jaintia*, Pts.I-III, Shillong, 1991, which is a political history of the Khasi-Jaintias. The first History of India in Khasi language was written by Jeebon Roy, an Extra. Assistant Commissioner who published, *History of India in Khasi*, Ri Khasi Press, Shillong 1900. The book has three sections on "Hindu", "Muhammadan" and British history of India bringing up the narrative to Lord Curzon's Viceroyalty.

Chapter VII

WRITINGS IN KHASI VERNACULAR PERTAINING TO SOCIO-POLITICAL ISSUES: A REVIEW

L.S. Gassah

With the ever increasing literature written in the Khasi vernacular for the last one hundred and fifty seven years, the task becomes more difficult for a layman like me to be able to comprehend over this wide ocean of knowledge. The Khasi literature in the from of a vernacular has progressed and developed in leaps and bounds covering almost all fields of literary works, especially in Social Sciences and Humanities like—Poetry, History Political History and Thought, Drama, Geography, Folktales and Folklore and a host of other academic disciplines.

On account of the vast canvas of Khasi literature written in vernacular language, this paper has a number of limitations. Also, this paper limits its coverage only to those areas dealing with socio-political issues. Even after limiting the scope of the paper to such issues, it is still incomplete. In one sense, this work is not only tentative but it can be said to be of an introductory nature.

Talking about socio-political issues as reflected through the published works in Khasi literature, we are still compelled to set aside for the time being, those writings that appeared in the form of poems, dramas, dialogues, folktales, etc. As far as possible we are trying to review in this first exercise only those writings that appeared in a prose form—that too, by taking into account only those serious works that have been published in book form.

The intellectuals (Scientists and Social Scientists) when they search knowledge about man and his environment, they examine the signs/symbols, any written words/drawings etc., to extract some information about the past to understand the present better. Broadly speaking, the period is divided into Pre-historic and Historic. Among the Khasi-Jaintia people, the pre-historic period is the most difficult one.

With the coming of the British, the Christian Missionaries followed. Thanks to the untiring efforts of the earlier Christian Missionaries like Thomas Jones and a host of others, the Khasi vernacular started taking shape in a written form. Though a long period of the initial years was spent on the translation of the *Bible* and other religious books, this period proved to be the most important humble beginning. Among the local pioneers, the name of Jeebon Roy (or Babu Jeebon Roy) and a few others appeared prominently in the list of those who contributed immensely in the growth and development of the Khasi vernacular.

Once the Khasi literature takes off from the ground, there is no going back. Rather we experienced its steady growth, development and improvement. The first attempt made by William Carey for translation of the Bible into Khasi by using the Bengali alphabet did not succeed. It was not, however, till the arrival of Thomas Jones of the Welsh Calvinistic Mission at Sohra on the 22nd June 1841, that a serious attempt was made to put the Khasi language in a written form by using the Roman alphabet. I.M. Simon is of the opinion that "he (Thomas Jones) his choice of the Roman alphabet for the writing of Khasi was not a haphazard decision. True, the London Missionary Society had made a beginning with the Bengali script, but the literature produced was imperfect in the sense that it was not acceptable as Khasi writing. It was only when Alexander Lish, the 18 year old missionary, was sent to these hills and resided within one dialect area, which by a happy coincidence happened to be the home of the Cherra dialect or

Ka Ktien Sohra that the writings produced by him for the first time made sense".[1]

Thomas Jones would appear to have been a man of strong convictions. As he was familiar with the Roman Alphabet only, and having started to learn Khasi, he realised that this Alphabet was suitable for the writing of this language. Among the first tasks Thomas Jones took up were the preparation of school books for beginners and the writing of religious literature, as well as the translation of the New Testament into Khasi.

Regarding the Political History of the Khasi-Jaintia people, there have been a number of books written and published. One of the earliest books on this subject is that of Dr.H. Lyngdoh—*Ki Syiem Khasi Bad Synteng* (1952) (Khasi and Jaintia *Syiems*). The book consists of 19 (nineteen) chapters dealing with the history and administration of all the Khasi-Jaintia Syiemships. The book is of great importance as it gives detailed information about the origin, development, geneology of the *Syiems* and the over-all administration of these Syiemships. Mention may be also made here of L.G. Shullai's book *Ki Hima Khasi* (the Khasi States, 1975). It deals with the formation of the Khasi States, their position and status before and after India's Independence, their signing of the Standstill Agreement and Instrument of Accession and the administration of these States. The book contains important and helpful information about the Khasi States. The Appendices provide additional imformation relating to the relationship between the Khasi States and the British as well as the Indian Union after Independence. Very recently, L.G. Shullai published two books—*Ka bri Hynniewtrep Bad Ka Sixth Schedule* (1998) (Khasi-Jaintia Hills and the Sixth Schedule) and *Ka Shillong Naduh 1863* (Part I & II) (1998) (Shillong since 1863). The former analyses the relationship between the erstwhile British Area (i.e. Jaintia Hills), the Khasi States and the Autonomous District Councils (ADCs) in Khasi-Jaintia Hills under the Sixth Schedule to the Indian Constitution. The Acts passed by the ADCs from time to time and their effects on the traditional institutions are also discussed. The latter deals in Part I with the Shillong Municipality and Shillong (Administered Area) Municipality. Part II discusses about the Cantonment Area of

Shillong and its historical and administrative development. As in his other books, the Appendices included in these books provide important sources of information. Students of Political Science and History will find the books to be of great help as sources of information.

On the socio-cultural issues, much literature in Khasi has been published dealing with the questions of traditions, customs and cultural practices relating to marriage, family and kinship as well as the changes that have appeared in the transitional period of the history of the people of Khasi and Jaintia Hills.

It is interesting to note that the Khasi books, especially those which are of recent publication, bring out a number of pertinent issues regarding the changing situation that appears in the Khasi-Jaintia society and how these changes have or might have their effects in the concept of family and kinship among the people and the society. The writers of these books also do not forget to bring to the notice of the readers how inter-marriage, especially with the non-Khasis, may lead to such knotty problems on the family, kinship and the entire gamut of clan relationship as well as the economic impacts due to such marital relationship outside the Khasi society.

The position, status and role of *Ka Khadduh* (youngest daughter) appear prominently in those books dealing with the socio-cultural issues. There are books not only on the status and role of women but men also especially that of *Knyi* (maternal uncle). What are the changes in the role of the maternal uncle due to the changing pattern of professions, job opportunities, when he has to be away to a distant place—far from his brothers, sisters, nephews, nieces, etc.? This and a host of other problems have now raised their heads in the changing situation. Few books have also discussed the different aspects of culture—including that of family, faith, social problems and the impact of western and other cultures on the Khasi-Jaintia society. Some authors in the form of poems, dramas, novels, etc. have raised the question of the future of the Khasi-Jaintia society. Where is the future of the Khasi-Jaintia society? Where do we go from here? Some such authors did try to suggest ways and means of how to get rid of the various problems faced by the society at large. The ever increasing number of books written in Khasi vernacular, does not only increase the quantity but also the quality and improvement of the language itself. This is a welcome trend in the writings in Khasi in the recent years.

On the issue of *Ka Niam Khasi* (Khasi traditional religion) a number of excellent books have been written and published. A good number of articles on this important issue have been written and published in different Journals, Souvenirs, Pamphlets and occasional papers. A few of such published works may be mentioned here—*Ka Niam Khasi* (1937; 1990) By Dr. H. Lyngdoh; *Ka Niam Ki Khasi* (1919; 1978) by Sib Charan Roy; *Ka Pomblang Nongkrem Bad Ka Thangsyiem Sohra* (1928) by Dr.H. Lyngdoh; *Ka Niam Khasi* by Jeebon Roy; *Ka Kitap Niam Khasi* by Rabon Sing and *Ka Kitap Jingphawar* by the same author; *U Khasi Ha La Ka Niam, Seng Khasi Souvenir* (published by Seng Khasi from time to time), *Ka Riti Jong Ka Ri Laiphew Syiem* (Part I & II) by G. Costa, etc.

These books or articles on *Ka Niam Khasi* provide such information on the basic tenets, practices, form and practice of rites and rituals, ceremonies, customs and usages in connection with the Khasi traditional religion and religious beliefs. Mention may be made also here of the discussions and analyses on the impact of Christianity on the people and the society at large.

It is also interesting to note here that books on folklore and folktales have a lot to contribute on the understanding of the Khasi-Jaintia history in general and the important aspects of religious rites and ceremonies that are still performed and celebrated by different *Raids*. The untiring efforts made by Donbok T. Laloo are worth mentioning. His contribution to Khasi literature has been enormous and to Khasi folklore is unsurpassed. His highly acclaimed work *Ka Sajer* is about the agrarian ceremony of *Raid Khatar–Nonglyngdoh* of Ri Bhoi district. The book is a veritable goldmine of information about the material culture, ethnography, religious beliefs and practices and a useful lexicographical information to the *Karew*, the indigenous people of the Bhoi area.[2]

On the socio-economic issues and problems faced by the Khasi-Jaintia society, there is no dearth of books. These issues could also be found in those books written on the history and culture of the Khasi-Jaintia people. Among the authors and their books on the socio-economic problems and drawbacks of the people, mention may be made here of a celebrated book by P.R. Mawthoh, entitled *Balei U Khasi Um Roi-Spah* (1967) (Glimpses of the Socio-Economic Drawbacks of the Khasis). The author has analysed in great detail the causes that led to the socio-economic drawbacks of the Khasis. In brief, he listed these causes as—false sense of pride and dignity, unemployment and unbalanced growth in trade and commerce, overconcentrated and suicidual competition, complacency or intertia and shortsightedness, vainful extravagance, lack of capital and unequal competition, lack of initiative and business enterprise. Besides these, there are problems like agriculture and agricultural practises, tools and implements, influx of village population to the towns, etc.. Having discussed these problems, the author suggested some ways and means how to overcome them, of which spread of education, co-operatives, cultivation of the habit of economical management of income, expenditure and savings, development of enterprise and initiative, development of the new means of communications, marketing facilities, etc., play an important role.

In the same spirit of discussion on the issues and problems of socio-economic backwardness, a number of books have been published. In general, these books take serious note of the situation that prevailed before and after India's Independence and how these two periods of history had effected the socio-economic conditions of the Khasi-Jaintia people. The authors discussed in their books about the flourishing trade and commerce in the pre-partition days, the extent of participation and involvement of the Khasi-Jaintia traders with their counterparts in the plains, in terms of trade and commerce especially that of Sylhet district, during those hectic days. Having made a comparative analysis between the pre and post partition days, many of these authors lamented of the lost opportunities as a result of the Partition of 1947. Thus, writings in Khasi vernacular pertaining to the economic problems of the Khasi-Jaintia people did find an appreciative attempt by many Khasi authors.

Of late, due to the formation of such an association known as 'Ka Synjuk Rympei Thymmai', a number of books on the socio-economic problems of the Khasi-Jaintia people have been written with a view to project the opinions of a certain school of thought. Some prominent members of this 'Synjuk' have even gone to the extent of questioning the age-old traditional practices of matrilineal system and inheritance of property. Some of these books were based on these two systems by trying to prove or disprove of the need for continuity and how the practices give rise to a number of social and economic problems. To sum up, they are of the strong opinion that one of the main causes of economic backwardness of the Khasi-Jaintia people is due to the practice of matrilineal system and the present system of inheritance or management of properties, especially that of ancestral property. The opinion of this school of thought is of course still debatable. But the very fact that some books have been written and published on this particular issue, speaks of the kind of socio-cultural and academic consciousness of the thinkers among the Khasi-Jaintia people. Such published works have enriched the literary culture of the people and their sensitivity to such topical tricklish issues, which in the past were discussed only in their hearths and homes. But now, they have realised that these kind of traditional practices do not help to inform the people at large, so these ideas have now been put in black and white for wider circulation of opinion and knowledge itself. As such literary works have been written in Khasi, even the rural population have the chance to read and build up their own opinion and judgement on their society which is undergoing a tremendous transformation in the transitional period. Such discussion seems to go on as long as the society continues to face such problems and we expect more such opinions in the years to come through the writings of different local scholars.

On the close heels of socio-economic problems, the question of land, land tenure system and land-use pattern among the Khasi-Jaintia people follows. Many thought – provoking published works by the Khasi authors have already come out. These books discuss such pertinent issues like land tenure system, land-use patterns, kinds/types of lands as prevailed in the society, the question of inheritance, rights over the land and its management, etc. While discussing about land, the question of forests, their use management, ownership, etc. also comes into the picture. The authors of these books do not of course forget to inform the readers about the role and constitutional status of the traditional institutions like the *Syiem, Lyngdoh, Doloi, Pator,* etc. as well as the new constitutional set up in the form of the Autonomous District Council and State Government in relation to the issue and problems of land and forests in the Khasi and Jaintia Hills.

In short, the quality and quantity of literature in the form of Khasi vernacular in all its genre has marched on ahead of many of the languages of the tribals of North-East India. The credit for such a steady growth and progress is due to the spirit of consciousness and concern about one's own people and society and the untiring efforts put in by many local writers and scholars. Their literary efforts have increased the quantity and raised the standard and quality of Khasi literature to a greater height in comparison with the progress made by the neighbouring tribal communities and their languages in the North-Eastern region. Language is a vehicle of social change and transformation. Khasi has survived for centuries in spite of its not having any script till comparatively recently. Khasi has preserved its basic identity while enriching itself by borrowing from other languages. It is a member of the Mon-Khmer family of languages spoken in South-East Asia and it therefore provides us with a useful link with these neighbours.

References

1. Simon, I.M.: 'A Tribute to Thomas Jones I' in Khasi Authors Society 150th. Anniversary of Khasi Literature, p. 25.
2. Kharmawphlang, D.L.: 'The Life and Works of Donbok T. Laloo' (Mimeograph), Symposium on Khasi Authors and their contributions, Department of Art and Culture, Government of Meghalaya, Shillong (held on 3–4 Nov., 98).

Chapter VIII

SOCIAL SCIENCES IN MIZO

Lianzela

Mizoram, which previously had three districts namely Aizawl, Lunglei and Chhimtuipui is now administratively divided into eight districts; Aizawl, Aizawl East, Aizawl West, Aizawl South, Aizawl North, Lunglei, Chhimtuipui and Chhimtuipui East. Mizoram literally translated means "Land of the Highlanders". Prior to 1972 Mizoram was one of the districts of Assam. She then became a Union Territory in 1972 and finally a State, the 23rd state of India in 1987.

Mizoram had its formal primary schools opened in villages in 1903, and first High School and College opened in 1944 and 1958 respectively. The State had a literacy percentage of 82.27 in 1991 which is the second highest in India. The State claims to have 89.94 percent literacy as on August 1996. The Educational Development Index (EDI) prepared by the Planning Commission, Government of India (Education Division) ranked Mizoram first followed by Goa and the third being Kerala. The parameters used for EDI are: investment in education, literacy achievement, universalisation of elementary education and availability of educational facilities. Mizoram had 341 recognised village libraries in 1998. The number has risen to 360 in 1999.

There have been quite a number of books written in vernacular language (Mizo) in the recent past in Mizoram. Number of books published in Mizo language in Mizoram since 1989 are as follows[1] -

Year	Number of Books in Mizo Language
1989	53
1990	55
1991	65
1992	85
1993	146
1994	166
1995	101
1996	122
1997	113
1998	102
Total	1008

The majority of the books published in recent years in Mizoram were written in Mizo language by different authors on diverse subjects. For example the new books in 1997 can be classified into six broad categories:

1.	Religion	31
2.	Language and Literature	30
3.	Biography	14
4.	History	9
5.	Science and Technology	4
6.	Others	25
	Total	**113**

The above classification will broadly be applicable for the previous years too. Most of the recent publications in Mizo language are on Mizo literature, folk tales, fiction and drama. Books on Christian family have also come out in significant numbers. Unfortunately books on Social Sciences are still few in the State till today. With the coming of Mizoram Publication Board (established 1996), giving grant in aids to the deserving writers/authors (of book) the situation is expected to improve in the near future. Besides, to promote publication of books Mizo Academy of Letters (MAL) gives Book of the year award to the best author since 1989. The award carries cash award and a citation. This award has promoted publication of books in vernacular language in the State of Mizoram.

Let me now try to analyse the availability of books in vernacular languages in Mizoram in Social Sciences.

Economics

Till recently majority of Mizo students did not want to study economics as they thought the same to be a difficult subject, next to mathematics. The trend is slightly different now. Till today books on economics written in vernacular language are but few. Students could bot get adequate reading material in Mizo language on Indian Economics, North Eastern Economy and Mizoram Economy etc. Following are some of the books on Economics written in Mizo language.

1. Rinawma, R.L. *Ram Mamawn Energy Tuakna Kawng*, Lalfakawma Ralte, Ramhlun 'N', Aizawl, 1995.
2. Lianzela *Kristiante leh Mahni Intodelh*, Khuangkungi Venghnuai, Aizawl, 1995.
3. Lawmtnanga *Thiaithar Hralhna* (Agricultural Marketing), M.C. Lalrinthanga, Khatla, Aizawl, 1997.
4. Thangmawia, H. *Industry Kailawn*, Techno Consultancy, 1998.
5. Lalmanzuala, M. *Zoram Kalsiam*, Sapthlengliana, Zarkawt, Aizawl, 1998.
6. Lalsawta *Budget Mipui Sum*, Senhri Publication, Aizawl, 1995
7. Lalchhuanliana (ed.) *Kristiante Rahbi Thar*, Synod Social Front Committee, 1991.
8. Remthanga, H. (ed.) *Hmasawnna Kawngpui* (Synod Social Front—16) Synod Social Front Committee, 1997.
9. Lalchhuana, R. *Japan Hlawhtlinna Thuruk*, Muanpuia, Aizawl, 1993.

The first of these books is about power and energy for Mizoram. Since the need of the day in Mizoram is enough supply of power and energy, the author who is an Indian Revenue Service Officer suggests measures to have sufficient power and energy supply in Mizoram. The second book is about self-sufficiency in foodgrain production etc. The book also highlights the economic development position of Mizoram. The book is a collection of Lianzela's articles on diverse subjects. No. 3 is about Agricultural Marketing in general and also with special reference to Mizoram. It is a very good book on the subject. The author is an officer in trade and Commerce Department in Mizoram. Serial No. 4 is about Industry—how to establish an industry, what kind of aids or assistance can be given etc. The author being in the Department for a number of years has in-depth knowledge of his subject matter. No.5 is about socio-economic development of Mizoram. Although it is not a research based writing, the book would be of immense help to the readers. The writer is a retired IAS officer who has a long and rich experience in Mizoram in the capacity of development Commissioner and later Chief Secretary of the State of Mizoram. *Budget Mipui Sum* is about the Budget (India and Mizoram). It is a small book. Since each terminology is clearly explained it would be a good book for the students of Economics at the School and even College (Junior) levels. The writer is a former MLA of Mizoram. No. 7 and 8 are books on socio-economic development. They are a collection of seminar papers written by selected resource persons on the chosen themes. Both are published by Synod Social Front Committee of the Mizoram Presbyterian Synod. There are other publications made by the Synod Social Front, which are quite relevant for economics students. But as they are rather small, 29 and 40 pages, they are intentionally excluded from the present study.

The last one in the section is a comparison of the economics of Japan and the U.S.A The main intention of the author is to highlight the cause of the rapid development of Japan economy. The author urges the people of Mizoram to follow the example of the Japanese.

History

Books on History can broadly be classified into three groups, viz., pure history, political history and church history. The following books are in the group of pure history:

1. Liangkhaia, Rev. — *Mizo Chanchin*, Hmingliana & Sons, Aizawl, 1984.
2. Zawla, K. — *Mizo Pi Pute an thlahte Chanchin*, K. Zawla, 1989 (5th edition)
3. Siama, V.L. — *Mizo History*, Lengchhawn Press, Khatla, Aizawl, 1991.
4. Zatluanga — *Mizo Chanchin*, Zasanga IPS, Aizawl, 1996.
5. Lalthangliana, B. (ed.) — *Mizo Lalropuite*, Vol. I, M.C. Lalrinthanga, Aizawl, 1996.
6. Dokhuma, James — *Hmanlai Mizo Kalphung*, J.D. Press Publication, 1996.
7. Vanlallawma, C. — *YMA History 1935–1995*, Central YMA, 1998.
8. Vanlalchhuanga — *Mizo leh Khuang*, Vanlalchhuanga Venghnuai, Aizawl, 1996.
9. Vanlallawma, C. — *Mizo Hnam Puipate*, Lengchhawn Press, Khatla, Aizawl, 1994.
10. Lianhmingthanga (ed.) — *Mizo Lal Ropuite*, Tribal Research Institute, Art & Culture Directorate, Aizawl, 1996.
11. Lalremsiama, F. — *Milu lak leh Vai Run Chanchin*, MCL Publication, Khatla, Aizawl, 1997.
12. Lalhmuaka — *Zoram History* (1800–1950), Lalhmuaka, Aizawl, 1992.
13. Lalsangzuali Sailo — *Sakhming Chullo*, AJBM Publication, Bungkawn, Aizawl, 1995.
14. Seletthanga — *Pi Pu Lenlai*, 1973.
15. Lalthangliana, B. — *Mizo Nun Hlui*, Part I (1982); Part II (1993)
16. Lalthangliana, B. — *History of Mizo in Burma*, Zawlbuk Agency, 1980.
17. Lalbiaknema, C. — *Kan Chenna Mizoram*, Synod Publication Board, 1995.
18. " — *Mizo Lal Ropuite*, Art and Culture Department, Govt. of Mizoram, 1997.
19. " — *Zofate Chan Chin*, Hualngo Literature & Culture Association, 1995.

Serial numbers 1 to 4 are pure history books and are the best books we have on Mizo history. The books are not written on research base but are written mainly from personal experiences. The writers are not historians themselves. They are not academicians in the strict sense. But their source materials are quite reliable.

The fifth book in this series is about Mizo Chiefs (Some of the greatest among the Mizo Chiefs). It is an edited volume. No. 6 is about Mizos, their customs, practices etc. No. 7 is about the maker of modern Mizos. No. 8 is about cultural history, the use and importance of the drum in the life and society of the Mizos. No. 9 is about the history of the Young Mizo Association, the largest voluntary organisation in Mizoram involving all the Youth of Mizoram. No. 10 is another book about the great Mizo chiefs. It is an edited volume.

Serial No. 11 is about head hunting. The early Mizos are often called headhunters. It also tells of the invasion into Cachar by the Mizos. It is one of the best books on the subject. The writer has an M.Phil. Degree and is a research scholar in history. This is written on the basis of his research submitted to the North-Eastern Hill University. No. 12 is about Mizoram history. No. 13 is again about some select and prominent Mizos who have contributed significantly in their respective fields. No. 14 is about the life and society of the Mizos in ancient time. No. 15 is also about the life style, custom, and practices of the Mizo people. No. 16 is about the history of Mizo in Burma of which there are not many books. Nos. 17, 18 and 19 are again on history of Mizoram published recently like other previous books. These are not written on research based study.

Political History

Under this group there are altogether seven books.

1. Thanglura, A. *Zoram Politic Lumlet Dan,* A Thanglura, 1948.
2. Saprawnga, C.H. *Ka Zinna Kawng,* Lalkungi Chanmari, Aizawl.
3. Lalsawia *Zoram Hminghmel,* Aizawl, 1996.
4. Lalrinthanga, M.C.*Zoram Politic 1976–1986,* Aizawl, 1993.
5. Chaltuahkhuma, *Political History of Mizoram (1920–1980),* 1981.

6. Lalrawnliana *Zoramin Zalenna a sual*, Vols. I to IV, Aizawl, 1995–97.
7. Biakchhunga*Hnam Kalsiam*, LV Arts, Chanmari, Aizawl, 1996.

The first in this category is about the political events and changes that have happened in Mizoram. The second and third in this category are more or less biographies. The authors, while projecting themselves in most of the political events of the time have highlighted the political history of the time. A serious reader can very well learn the political history of Mizoram from these books. No. 4 is confined mainly to the period between 1976–1986 and is quite specific about the political events and situation of the period. No. 5 is a political history for the period 1920–1980. No. 6 is about the Mizo National Front (MNF) movement in Mizoram, the insurgency, the peace talks etc. There are four volumes in this study. No. 7 is also a book on political history of Mizoram. From research point of view it may not be a very good book but for collecting information to know the political situation of the time, it may be a valuable book.

Church History

Under this group there are a number of books that are readily available. But most of these books are not standard books as they are written by lay people who are not trained as historians. At the local church level there are church history books written by the local church members. But these are not included now. Books selected for this category are those that cover the whole Mizoram or the larger denominations.

1. Saiaithanga : *Mizo Kohhran Chanchin*, The Mizo Theological Literature Committee, 1969.
2. Malsawmi : *Mizoram Presbytarian Kohhran Hmeichhe Chanchin*, Synod Publication Board, 1993.
3. Laltluangliana, K. : *Kristian Thalai Pawl Chanchin*, Synod Publication Board, Aizawl, 1993.

4. Hluna, J.V. : *Mizoram Welsh Missionary te Chanchin*, Synod Publication Board, 1993.
5. Sangkhuma, Z.T. : *Missionary te hnuhma*, Lalrinthanga, Aizawl, 1995.
6. Lalhmuaka : *Zoram Thim ata Engah*, Synod Publication Board, 1988.
7. Dokhuma, James : *Zoram Tualto Kohhran Chanchin*, James Dokhuma, Aizawl, 1977.
8. Vanlalchhuanga : *An Zirtirnate*, Vol. I and II, Vanlalchhuanga Venghnuai, Aizawl, 1984, 1985.
9. Darchhawna : Church History, Linkman Publication Titagarh 24 Parganas,(N), 1998.
10. Lalrinawmi Ralte : *Mizo Nula Huaisen Marterte*, Lalriliani, Aizawl, 1994.

The first book in this category is written by a Pastor and is one of the best books for Church history in Mizoram. Since it is one of the pioneer books in the subject, it does not cover the recent period. The second, third and fourth are Gospel Centenary Series of Mizoram Presbyterian Church Synod. No. 2 is about the Presbyterian Church Women Fellowship of Mizoram. The writer had deep involvement in the Fellowship and could write the story effectively. The same is the case with serial No. 3. This is about Christian Youth Fellowship in Mizoram. One can clearly see the Youth activities, its role in the Church and its role in supporting the cause of evangelism. No. 4 is about the history of Welsh Missionaries in Mizoram. No. 5 is also about Mission work done by missionaries in Mizoram for the cause of the gospel.

Serial No. 6 is about how the Gospel transformed the lives of the Mizo people. The Gospel light was brought to Mizo people thereby enlightening the people in various ways. No. 7 is about the indigenous churches in Mizoram. These are churches that are not established by Mizos themselves because of various reasons. No. 8 is about Heretics and their teachings in Mizoram. It has two volumes. The two volumes are written on the basis of personal interviews and collection of important data on the subject. Serial No. 9 is church history in general and is written by one of the historians. The book is one of the best books for Church history we have in Mizo language. No.

10 is about the lives and work of Mizo Women Missionaries who gave their lives for the cause of the Gospel.

Other writings on History, particularly history of Christianity etc. which found a place in the compilation made by the Faculty of Aizawl Theological College (ATC) are:

1. Bawla, R.L. : *Burma Ram Presbyterian Kohhran Chanchin*, (History of Presbyterian Church of Burma), Tahan: Synod Literature Committee, 1975.
2. Hawla, V. : *Mizoram Chhim leh Hmar Missionary te*, (The Missionaries of North and South Mizoram) Aizawl Nazareth Press, 1970.
3. Lalauva, R. : *Mizoram Kohhran 7 te Chanchin leh an Kaihhruai Dan*, (The History of Seven Churches in Mizoram and their Practices) Aizawl Nazareth, 1985.
4. Lalbiaktluanga : *Uar Bik Nei Pawlte* (The Denominations with Special Emphasis) Aizawl, Synod Literature Committee, 1977.
5. Lalchhuanliana : *India Ram Kohhran Chanchin*, (Indian Church History) Aizawl, Theological College, 1981.
6. Lalhmuaka : *Zoram Kristian Hmasa Tihduhdahna*, (Persecutions faced by Early Mizo Christians), Aizawl, Synod Publication Board, 1985.
7. Lalhmuaka : *Zoram Thim ata Engah*, (From Darkness to light), Aizawl, Synod Publication Board, 1988.
8. Liandawla Hnamte : *Mizo Kohhran Hrang hrangte Chanchin, Rin dan leh Inrelbawl dan* (Beliefs and Administration of the Various Mizo Churches), Shillong, Ell Cee Hnamte, 1989.
9. Liangkhaia : *Kohhran Hrang Hrang Chanchin*, (The History of Different Denominations), Aizawl, Welsh Mission Book Room, 1953.
10. Malsawma, J. : *Zonun*, (The Life of the Mizos), Aizawl Literature Society, 1977.

Political Science

There are not many books on Political Science. Some may be categorised as political economy while others may be put as public administration etc.

1. Vanlawma, B. : *Ka Ram leh Kei,* Lalrinthanga and S.P.H. Zalen Cabin, 1965.
2. Lalnithanga, P. : *Civil Service leh Kei,* P. Lalnithanga, Aizawl, 1988.
3. Sapa Ronald : *Zoram thar Vanlalzawma,* 1998.
4. Biakmawia, C. : *Mizoram Politics,* Synod Social Front Committee, 1992.
5. Lalkhawliana, Zohmangaiha & Laltlunagliana, K. : *Mizoram Politics and Economy Mizo Kristiante thlir dan,* (Consultation Papers), YMCA. Aizawl, Mizoram, 1989.
6. Rualkhuma, Hmar : *India Sawrkar leh Politics.*
7. Keivom, L. : *Zoram Khawvel.*

No. 1 in this category is an autobiography type of book. The author, while narrating his own story clearly indicates about the politics in Mizoram, Assam, etc. No. 2 is about Public Administration. The writer is an IAS Officer. He has written from his personal experiences, his involvement and the role in public/civil administration etc. Serial No. 3 is about political economy and also public administration. It is the story of the Public Administration in Mizoram, the success and failures in Mizoram Government/Ministry and measures to improve the same. It is an informative book. No. 4 is written on the basis of seminar papers. The Synod Social Front Committee requested some talented people who know the subject thoroughly to write papers on Mizoram politics. These papers have been published in a book form. No. 5 is again a consultation paper on Mizoram politics and economy organised by Young Men Christian Association in Mizoram. No. 6 is about Indian Government and Politics. The writer is a college lecturer. The book helps understand principles of political science etc. The last one (No. 7) is about nation building. The author wrote four volumes on the same title but only the fourth volume is included under Social Science subjects under Political Science.

References

1. *Sabereka Khuangkaih,* April and May 1998, p. 48.

Chapter IX

DEVELOPMENT OF TENYIDIE: A FOCUS ON SOCIAL SCIENCES

D. Kuolie

No one will deny that every racial stock or an established nation has its own history as well as their basic human and social phenomenon that lies open for academic challenges. Modern society around the world has shown a fast transitory trend at the influence of science and technology, making the universe becoming, in the words of our late Prime Minister Jawaharlal Nehru, "smaller and smaller." However, the academic research fields, instead of becoming narrower, are becoming wider and wider as numerous disciplines of human learning are set on foot to the scholars. Whereas science and technology seek to cater human needs and minimise human problems by way of industrialisation and engineering creativity in the form of economic expansion, the study of social sciences tries its best to bring the people of diverse groups into closer contact with an objective of bringing them into closer relationship amidst the vast ocean of varied global community. Indeed, our human learning process is objectively fulfilling various aspects of human knowledge at micro-level for a fuller macro-built. It is obvious that any integral study can hardly be a success without the minutest consideration. As such, the study of Tenyidie literature, I hope, will certainly provide some new dimensional force with its hidden values in various branches of social sciences. It will also provide some significant specimens to the social fabric of the Nagas in a larger context.

It would be proper to mention something of the historical background of the development of Tenyidie literature before entering into the core of the subject matter. Tenyidie literary development, historically, goes back to the contribution of American missionaries. It was in the later part of the 19th century that the British India took domination of some part of Nagaland. Under the British colonial protection the American missionaries entered into the land of the Nagas and established their missionary centres. Their objective was to spread Christianity but it was an impossible task for them due to the absence of language communication facility. The need to impart literacy education, therefore, became necessary. A school was first opened where Assamese was the medium of instruction. This failed to attract the Nagas. Rev. C.D. King, one of the earliest American missionaries learnt Tenyidie. His successor, Sydney White Rivensburg too learnt Teynidie and started writing some reading primers in the Roman script on an experimental basis. The experiment showed an impressive result and that was the beginning of Tenyidie literature. The promotion continued with encouragement from the British administrators. In order to strengthen, Rev. J.E. Tanquist constituted a literary body called *Angami Literature Committee* (Tenyidie was formerly called Angami Languauge) which was approved by the then Deputy Commissioner of Naga Hills, C.R. Pawsey. Most of the earlier books were reading texts, *Bible* translations and hymnal translations. The reading texts included short stories, folklore, poetry, history, geography, health, arithmetic, language structures, idioms etc.

The progress of Tenyidie literature was adversely affected due to the outbreak of the World War II. Later a fierce battle was fought at Kohima between the British and the Japanese supported Indian National Army. The schools and its academic belongings were burnt down in 1944. The reviving stage was not long lived. It was shattered again with the outbreak of the Naga revolution for independence in the year 1956. The progress of Tenyidie literature could be revived and stabilised again only in the early 1970s when the Angami Literature Committee was nomenclated into Ura Academy. The Ura

Academy now stands not only as the apex body of literary development but also the highest institution and agency for promotion of other branches of learning in Tenyidie.

Etymologically, *Tenyidie* means 'the language of the Tenyimia' group of the Nagas; genetically the generations from 'Tenyiu.' The Tenyimia group includes the following Naga tribes—the Angamis, Chakhesangs, the Zeliangs and the Rengmas of Nagaland State and the Maos and Poumai of Senapati district of Manipur State. Tenyidie is the standard variety spoken around Kohima, the capital of Nagaland. Tenyidie was recognised as a Modern Indian Language in 1963 by the Secondary Board of Education, Assam, and students were offered the facility to appear the High School Leaving Certificate Examination with Tenyidie as a subject. However, it took another twenty-five years before the language was given recognition for the higher classes. In 1988 Tenyidie literature was introduced at the Pre-University level. Although late, the progress was impressive as today it has reached the post graduate level. The Ura Academy is indeed, indebted to the North Eastern Hill University and the Nagaland University for encouraging the development of this Naga language.

Since the inception of Ura Academy various activities in the field of education have been taken up. Apart from offering various academic courses such as Certificate, Diploma, B.A. and M.A. (Tenyidie), workshops, and seminars were conducted. Dramatic performance, cultural shows and western music are also conducted at regular intervals. In the process, many of the traditional knowledge and values were revived and promoted. Most of the activities taken by Ura Academy are recorded and published in its monthly journal, *Ura Dze*. Apart from the writings of literature as art, literature on social sciences, health and other human aspects have been developed to some extent. A brief account of the social science literature is given hereunder.

There are ancient historical events in oral literature, yet as explained earlier, due to lack of diachronic literature our account will begin only from the 19th century onward. One of the earliest books on history in Tenyidie is *U Runa Kechuu Naga Hills Dze* published in 1937, and written by Lhoulienyu. In this book, a brief historical account of the following is made:

1. The country of the Nagas prior to the colonial rule.
2. The early phase of contact between the Nagas and the British.
3. The invasion of Kohima by Manipur King Gambhir Singh.
4. A series of British attacks on Khonoma—1844, 1849, 1850, and 1879.
5. British attack on Mezoma—1849, 1876.
6. British invasion of Kenoma, Mao and Kikruma—1851
7. The second invasion of Mao—1866
8. The transfer of British military headquarters from Chumukedima to Kohima—1876
9. The last battle against the British colonalism in 1879 by about 14 villages.
10. The history of Ahom Kings; the colonial domination over Assam
11. Though brief, the ancient history of India such as the Aryans, Buddhism and Jainism, the Maurya empire, the Kushan kings, Harshavardhana and the Gupta period is covered. The entrance of the Muslims beginning from Mahamud Ghazni and Muhammad Ghori to the Mughal period is discussed. The coming of English to India; the East India Company; the beginning of colonial rule; the Viceroys of India is briefly noted. In the revised edition, a chapter on India's Independence and the leaders of India such as Dr Rajendra Prasad, Dr S. Radhakrishnan, Mahatma Gandhi, Jawaharlal Nehru, and Subhas Chandra Bose was added.

Shurhozelie, President, Ura Academy, a prolific writer of Tenyidie literature has published the whole historical accounts of the World War II in three volumes entitled *Kijuru Kneieu Bouhou*.

The development of literature, other than in literary field, many attempts are yet to be done. Many of the works in social sciences are in need of further elaboration or detailed study. Except in the seminar papers and few attempts many are not classified in terms of respective disciplines such as sociology, anthropology, political science, public admini-stration, economics and commerce. However, the academic attempts made on social sciences chapter are given in outline for information to the readers.

1. Migratory routes, settlement and establishment of villages.
2. Occupation and life style of the Nagas.
3. War adventures, war and treaties.
4. Weapons.
5. Myths and legends.
6. Understanding of signs of natural phenomena.
7. Traditional songs, poetry and music.
8. Social structure and their relationship.
9. Social life and social education.
10. Various stages of personal life.
11. Economic life and the processes of production; division of labour between sexes; classification of personal status on the basis of wealth.
12. Housing engineering.
13. Costumes and designs.
14. Games and sports, hunting and recreations.
15. Culture—Honesty, love and hospitability, manner and behaviour, politeness and action is personal as well as social.
16. Judicial—Land and other properties; inheritance, settlement of disputes; civil and criminal laws.
17. Village Administration: Administrators; recognition of individual as leader and selection for village administrations. Role and responsibilities of a leader and the responses of the citizens.
18. Festivals—Major and minor festivals; festivals and religion; Gate-pulling and monoliths.
19. Religion, belief and faith—processes of ritualisation on (a) human life (from birth to death); (b) domestic animals and (c) other properties; (d) to fellow friends and enemies; Individual and social ritual observation.
20. Proverbs and wisdoms.

Conclusion

To fulfil the dream of better society many people want as well as talk about a transformation. The present generation of today's world has tasted the impact of science and technology with both its positive and negative aspects. The forces, whether natural or non-natural that entangle human life indeed seem to be unique and hence difficult to overcome easily and wholly. However, there are ways and means that can deride the unwanted forces within our society. The promotion of studies in social sciences by way of research in tradition, refining and reviving may lay greater force in transforming the contemporary society. For the purpose, investigation of various cultures and traditions in unexposed society may find greater contribution.